An
Introduction
TO
YOUTH
MINISTRY

Wesley Black

**BROADMAN
& HOLMAN
PUBLISHERS**

Nashville, Tennessee

© Copyright 1991 • Broadman Press
All Rights Reserved
4232-44

ISBN: **0-8054-1869-5**
Dewey Decimal Classification: 259.23
Subject Headings: YOUTH MINISTRY // CHURCH WORK WITH YOUTH
Library of Congress Catalog Number: 90-20058

Printed in the United States of America

Library of Congress Cataloging-in-Publication Data

Black, Wesley.
  An introduction to youth ministry / Wesley Black
  p. cm
  Includes bibliographical references.
  ISBN **0-8054-1869-5**
  1. Church work with youth. I. Title.
  BV4447.B57 1991
  259'.23—dc20   90-20058
                                          CIP

00 01 15 14 13 12 11

To Sandi
My wife, my best friend

To Clay and Melissa
Our two children, my greatest challenges
and greatest sources of joy

To Mom and Dad
Who have given so much

Contents

Preface

On a warm summer night during youth camp I felt God's Spirit touch my life with a sense of calling into Christian vocational ministry. As a high school boy I did not fully know all that God had in store for me. But I responded to that call and began a journey of faith that eventually found purpose and calling in youth ministry.

I grew up in a small town in East Texas. The good people of Calvary Baptist Church were my friends, teachers, and models. My parents, Alvin and Bennie Black, took our small youth group to youth rallies, hayrides, and associational youth events. Almost every Sunday night ended with a gang of teenagers eating popcorn in the living room of our home or crowded into our car to go eat hamburgers. Although we did not have a youth minister, I was surrounded by people who loved, cared for, taught, and invested themselves in the small group of teenagers in our church.

The years have brought many memories. Among the sweetest is the joy of serving God in youth ministry. The relationships with youth, parents of youth, volunteer youth leaders, and church staff with whom I have served are God's precious gifts to me.

I presently serve as a seminary professor teaching students about youth ministry. My academic study includes a master's and doctorate, specializing in youth education in the church. My pursuit of study in this field has opened the door to the richness and expanse of youth ministry and reminded me of how much more there is to learn.

Youth ministry is more than an academic interest to me. Twenty-five years of youth ministry have only whetted my appetite in this field. My experiences as a high school band director, youth minister, and youth minister with music responsibilities have led to a greater appreciation for all youth leaders—both church staff youth ministers and volunteer youth leaders—who serve faithfully in youth ministry.

Some of my most exhilarating days have been those spent as a youth minister with teenagers in my own family. Such youth ministry may be challenging, but it is never dull!

Any attempt at saying thanks places one in danger of overlooking someone. But I must express my sincere gratitude to my family for their support and encouragement in this project. My wife, Sandi, has been my partner in ministry, encourager, prodder, and greatest prayer warrior. Our two adolescents, Clay and Melissa, have been most understanding when Dad was in the study writing and could not spend time with them. They are the living vessels of my hopes and dreams for the future.

My hope is for all those youth ministers, present and future, who read this book, to catch a vision of inclusive youth ministry that is *with* youth, parents of youth, all volunteer leaders with youth, and other church staff members. Further, that such a youth ministry, biblically grounded and resident in the family of God called church, will be able to carry out Christ's command to "make disciples of all the nations."

We can faithfully participate in all the joys, victories, challenges, disappointments, and successes of youth ministry because Jesus is "with [us] always, even to the end of the age" (Matt. 28:20).

Part 1
Foundations of Youth Ministry

1

A Theology for Youth Ministry

Youth ministry is a critical part of the mission of a church. Youth have the unique position of being the people of God today and the promise of God for tomorrow. While it once was considered adequate for a church to look upon its youth as the "church of tomorrow," that view is no longer sufficient. A church that takes seriously its mission must consider its ministry with youth today.

Why does our church need to do anything for those teenagers? Why don't we just give them a bus and the vacant house next door and let them do their thing? Why should the pastor be concerned with what the youth are doing? Isn't that the job of the youth sponsors or the youth minister?

These questions call for more than another program to entertain the youth. They cry for attention to the nature of Christian ministry. A church must do more than keep youth too busy to sin if it is to fulfill its mission.

Theological Building Blocks

Recently I had some repair work done on my house. The foundation had begun to settle and some cracks were appearing in the walls. The concrete slab had been built, not on sinking sand, but on clay that shrunk or expanded according to the moisture in the soil. The result was a foundation that was not firm enough to support my house.

The foundation repair crew sank steel rods into the ground around my house until they reached bedrock. Then they attached the foundation to those steel rods and brought my house up to level. The house then was sitting on bedrock, a much better support than the surrounding clay soil that was always changing.

Youth ministry should also be built upon a more substantial foundation than the whims of contemporary culture. The motives that shape our philosophy of youth ministry must be built on the solid bedrock of biblical theology. The following building blocks are some of the key elements of a solid foundation for youth ministry.

Building Block 1: A Biblical Focus

The Bible is God's authoritative revelation of Himself. Teenagers are moving into a stage of intellectual maturity in which they can begin to grasp some of the great themes of life. They gain new mental muscles and are intrigued by their new intellectual prowess. Along with the ability to argue, question, and debate with their parents, they also tend to question matters of faith and belief. The faith of parents and childhood must give way to a personalized, mature faith.

During this period of questioning and searching, the Bible stands as the only sure, authoritative word on matters of faith and belief. It is the inspired word from the Creator-Redeemer God (2 Tim. 3:16). Philosophies and fads may come and go but God's Word remains (Isa. 40:8).

If youth look to their own changing values or to the direction of others without relying on the authoritative Word of God, they are standing on shaky foundations.

The Bible plays a central role in all that grows out of authentic ministry with youth. Regular Bible studies, biblical content in youth events, times of sharing biblical truths, and purposes and organizing themes that grow out of the Bible are marks of youth ministry built on a biblical foundation. While every youth ministry event will not have a biblical proof text; every event, program, and activity will have a relationship to biblical faith as its ultimate reason for being. *Youth ministry must be built upon a solid foundation of biblical faith.*

Building Block 2: Grounded in God

God is the Creator, Redeemer, and Sustainer of all humankind. Teenagers are often seen as problems or objects of ministry. Teenagers are first and foremost human beings created in the image of God (Gen. 1:26). Though created in God's image, all people have chosen sin rather than God (Rom. 3:23). God in turn offers redemption in the form of the free gift of eternal life for all who will accept it (6:23). Teenagers, like all humans, need this free gift of salvation.

Only God can redeem us. Good works, education, philosophy, or psychology cannot save us. Only belief in the Creator-Redeemer God can assure us of the right relationship with God.

Youth ministry is God's work among teenagers and their families. God, as Creator, cares for all people, young and old. Teenagers are created with the innate ability to communicate with their creator God. As Redeemer, God is busy reaching out to all people with the good news of hope and salvation. As Sustainer, He constantly encourages, lifts up, and empowers His servants to do the work to which they are called (Phil. 2:13; Heb. 13:21). *Youth ministry is built upon a solid foundation, grounded in God as the Creator, Redeemer, and Sustainer.*

Building Block 3: People Need a Right Relationship with God

Adolescence is a time of searching as youth pledge fidelity in identity-shaping ways. In this process they encounter many questions concerning their relationships—to self, others, and ultimately God. In sorting through the decisions, they seek to answer two questions: Who am I and Whose am I? Those who have never professed faith in Jesus Christ—who have not yet settled the question of whose am I?—present two challenges for youth leaders.

First, youth who have grown up in Christian homes may be familiar with the terms of faith and the language of grace. They may be all too accustomed to the movement of God among people. Youth who have grown up beside the work of God, but who have never professed their own faith in Him, may be like the Hebrew people in the desert who forgot about the provisions of God (Ex. 6). They face the task of seeing God in new, fresh ways and determining for themselves their relationship to the faith of their families.

Second, youth who are not church oriented may be either fascinated or bored with Christianity. They may be intrigued by the mysteries of faith and truly interested in hearing the message of salvation. Or, they may be curious of Christianity like they are of Eastern mystic religions or cult groups. Those who are bored with the church may be reacting to insincere religious practices or the hypocrisy of some high-profile personalities.

These attitudes offer challenges to youth leaders. We must help youth struggle with the questions of faith and fidelity in sincere, authentic ways. Youth ministry offers the setting and context for teenagers to hear the message of salvation and accept the free gift of God through Jesus Christ (Rom. 6:23).

Evangelism should not be seen as one of the alternative activities of a church's youth ministry. It is the energy that flows through all we do. The message that people are lost without Christ (3:23) and in need of a right relationship with Him must flavor the blend of all youth ministry goals, projects, programs, and activities. *Youth ministry seeks to carry the message of salvation in appropriate ways to all youth.*

Building Block 4: The Church Is the Basic Unit of Ministry

God has chosen to work through churches to carry His message to the world (Matt. 16:18). Youth ministry must recognize this relationship and constantly seek ways to incorporate youth ministry into the total ministry of the church body. The youth group is not a separate world of ministry. It is integrally linked to the body of Christ—the church.

Youth who are members of the church are, in fact full members of the body of Christ. There is no difference theologically between the fourteen-year-old and the forty-year-old member. Youth who are Christians have been gifted and called to ministry and should be involved in the work of the church. Fellow members should seek to encourage youth and accept them into full membership in all areas of church life.

There is, however, a tremendous developmental difference between youth and other generations in the church. Youth ministry must seek creative ways to address the issues and challenges facing youth today. *Youth ministry is part of the total ministry of a church.*

Building Block 5: Recognize Developmental Processes

Teenagers are different from children and adults. They are no longer children but not yet adults. They stand with one foot in each world, in the awkward zone of adolescence.

Jesus gives us a model for relating to people at their level of understanding. As He taught the twelve, gradually revealing more and more of Himself as their understanding developed, He shows us today the necessity for teaching adolescents at their own level of understanding. He delegated responsibilities and involved the disciples in ministry, not all at once, but as they were prepared and willing to accept the tasks. Finally, Jesus ascended into heaven and left His followers to carry out the Great Commission.

Youth can be taught, equipped, and involved in the work of ministry. They can take on positions of leadership and be held accountable for their actions. They can understand, with growing awareness, the deep mysteries of the faith. But, they are adolescents, and those who minister to youth must consider the developmental maturity and react with loving care and nurture. Those who guide youth should remember they will not be mature, spiritually or otherwise, beyond their adolescent development. *Youth ministry recognizes the developmental uniqueness of adolescents.*

Building Block 6: Parents Are Responsible for Religious Training

Parents and family are important in ministry with youth. The family of Jesus observed the religious traditions of their day by traveling to Jerusalem for the annual observance of Passover (Luke 2:41-52). Even though there were some tense moments when the earthly parents of

Jesus, like their modern counterparts, did not understand the actions of their son, He still remained in right relationship with them.

Parents have a responsibility for the spiritual nurture of their children. Proverbs 22:6 says, "Train up a child in the way he should go." Ephesians 6:1-4 continues a discourse on family relationships with the admonition, "Fathers, do not provoke your children to anger; but bring them up in the discipline and instruction of the Lord" (v. 4).

Deuteronomy 6:4-5 (the Shema) contains the most revered words in Hebrew Scripture (cf. Mark 12:28-31). It was not unusual for young Hebrew children to hear these words so often that they knew them before they knew their parents' names. It is no coincidence that verses 6-7 immediately follow the Shema. Parents are instructed to teach the things of God to their children diligently, not just by sending them to church, but also in the normal routines of family life.

Youth ministry must consider the role of parents in the spiritual nurture of their teens. Youth ministers who ignore the parents of youth are building a ministry on a shaky theological foundation. *Youth ministry seeks ways for church and homes to be mutually supportive.*

Building Block 7: Youth Leaders Are Called to Minister

Adults volunteer to guide youth for a variety of reasons. Some sense the leadership of God to serve Him through youth ministry. Others sometimes work with youth for less noble reasons.

The distinguishing factor in biblical youth ministry is a sense of calling to ministry with youth. To minister—to serve—indicates a willingness to give rather than to receive. Those who work in youth ministry in order to receive—good strokes, power, relief from guilt, or escape from personal problems—will not find joy and satisfaction in their service. Only those who have sensed a call to serve God through youth ministry, who love and care for youth, and who are willing to prepare themselves for the task will taste the joy of service in youth ministry. *Youth ministry depends on the leadership of those called to minister.*

Building Block 8: God Calls Some to Specific Ministry with Youth

The New Testament does not specifically mention the church staff position of youth minister. However, there are many ministerial positions in modern churches that are not mentioned in the New Testament but are still valid.

God calls people for specific tasks (Moses, Nehemiah, Paul, and so forth) or for certain areas of ministry. These areas of ministry call for a response from the people of God to use the gifts and talents given by the Holy Spirit in furthering the kingdom of God. The gifts mentioned in

Romans 12, 1 Corinthians 12—14, and Ephesians 4 serve as striking examples of the gifts needed to serve effectively in modern youth ministry.

Youth ministers should not see their position as limited by their age. God has used people of every generation to do His will, and people of every age can serve as youth ministers. If God has gifted and called someone to serve Him in youth ministry, then age should not be a factor in responding to that call. *Youth ministry is an authentic calling, not a stepping-stone to another ministry.*

Building Block 9: Youth Are to Be Involved in Ministry

Both the Old and New Testaments provide examples of youthful servants of God. David was too young to accompany his older brothers to fight in the war (1 Sam. 17), but he led the army of Saul and the Israelites to victory against Goliath and the Philistines. David recognized the battle as more than a clash of military force. He boldly said, "You come to me with a sword, a spear, and a javelin, but I come to you in the name of the Lord of hosts, the God of the armies of Israel, whom you have taunted" (v. 45).

John Mark was eager to accompany his cousin Barnabas and the fiery evangelist Paul on their first missionary journey. In youthful exuberance, however, he did not count the costs of commitment the journey required and left the group to return home (Acts 13:13). This so angered Paul that he refused to allow John Mark to accompany him on the next missionary journey (16:36-39). The relationship with Barnabas turned out to be redemptive, however, and Paul later requested the company of John Mark (2 Tim. 4:11) because he had become "useful . . . for service." This same John Mark probably wrote the second Gospel.

The young king of the Old Testament and the author of the New Testament Gospel were both young servants of God. They had been called by God and encouraged by others to find their place of service in God's family. It should be this way with youth today. *Youth can be involved in meaningful ways in ministry.*

Building Block 10: Purpose of Youth Ministry

Why does a church need to be concerned with youth ministry? Is it enough to plan some activities that appeal to youth? Is a youth minister really only a baby-sitter for teenagers?

These questions probe the heart of youth ministry. A consistent, effective youth ministry demands answers that are biblically sound.

The parting words of Jesus to His disciples recorded in Matthew 28:18-20 and Acts 1:8 provide the Great Commission to followers of

Christ today. We are to make disciples. We are to teach them to observe all that Jesus commanded. We are to be witnesses for Christ, through the power of God's Holy Spirit, throughout the world.

The purpose of youth ministry follows the purpose of the church in the world. We are to point youth toward God and help them become involved in the Great Commission. Youth ministry can help teenagers reach, teach, obey, and witness for Christ in their world and beyond. *The purpose of youth ministry is to point youth toward God and help them become involved in the Great Commission.*

2

Ministry as Servant Leadership

The climax of Jesus' earthly ministry was at hand and the disciples were gathered for the Passover meal. Though they had been with Him for three years, the disciples still missed the point Jesus had taught them so often. Even as He told them of His impending suffering and death (Luke 22:14*ff*), they were more concerned about who was the greatest among them (v. 24).

Questions of power, authority, and greatness had perplexed the group on several occasions (see Matt. 18:1-5; 20:20-28; Mark 9:33-37; 10:32-45; Luke 9:46-48). Jesus must have wondered about the leadership potential of these who were to take up His ministry after the ascension. The time had come for one last lesson in leadership.

The group had entered the room from the dirt streets that were usually collections of filth cast off by travelers, raw sewage, manure, and mud. Since the men were barefoot or wearing only simple leather thongs, it was common courtesy for a slave to wash the feet of guests before they ate supper.

As Jesus looked around the group, no one was willing to do the task usually done by servants. John 13 recounts the great lesson in love and leadership as Jesus wrapped a towel around Himself, filled a basin with water, and got down on hands and knees to wash the feet of the disciples. He acted out the words about greatness and servanthood He had uttered so often before. Those who want to be greatest must first want to be servants.

It was more than a lesson in simple humility. It was a lesson that summarized His earthly ministry. It was a lesson that previewed the love He was about to demonstrate by dying on the cross. It was a lesson in love and leadership that disciples down through the ages must understand if they are to follow the model of leadership given by Jesus.

The disciples had understood authority that came from those with power to command and be served. The rulers and wealthy leaders were able to intimidate and coerce. The disciples pictured themselves

20

with this authority in the kingdom of God. But Jesus had different plans.

Those who are greatest in the kingdom of God achieve that greatness by being servants. To minister is to serve, and those who would be first in God's kingdom must picture themselves as servants of God and the family of God.

This may lead to some misconceptions of servanthood. First, it does not imply that a Christian leader must be a slave to the whims of others. Rather, Christian leadership means being bound to God in service and love—willing to serve Him as He sees fit. This service is expressed in loving ways to believers and unbelievers in order to convey the message of God's love for the world.

A second misconception is that servanthood means waiting until someone else gives direction. The servant simply responds to needs of the moment. Again, Christian leadership receives direction from God, it does not simply wait for incidents that dictate responses.

Two characteristics of Christian leadership can be seen in Jesus' ministry. The first is represented by the words "to send" and the other by the words "to serve."[1] Jesus described Himself as being sent by the Father (Matt. 15:24; Mark 9:37; Luke 9:48; John 3:17; 5:36; 6:29). In turn, Jesus sent the twelve (Matt. 10:5; Mark 3:14; 6:7; Luke 9:2; John 4:38) and the seventy (Luke 10:1). Those who received these disciples received Him who sent them in the same manner that those who received Christ also received the Father who sent Him. Modern disciples are sent as servants of God to do His will and be ministers through servanthood to others.

Jesus also emphasized service as a fundamental characteristic of ministry. He pointed to Himself (Luke 22:27; John 13:13-15) as the model for the disciples. As Teacher and Lord, He washed the disciples' feet as a symbol of servant leadership. To follow His example, they had to be willing to serve each other. Greatness in Christian ministry is not measured in outward rank or coercive power but in proportion to service (Matt. 20:25-28; Mark 10:42-45; Luke 22:24-27).

Youth ministry is also a sending and serving ministry. Those who lead youth ministry must do so out of a sense of being sent to this particular area of ministry. They lead youth to hear and respond to the sending call of God. Their ministry is one marked by service to God and other people. They lead youth to follow the example lived out before them and ultimately to follow the example Christ has given for servant leadership.

A youth minister friend confided that he felt used and manipulated by his pastor and those in power in the congregation. Though he tried to please them by doing all the menial tasks that came up, there were times he wished for more power or authority to combat the stress he felt.

Both the youth minister and the others were missing the example Jesus gave for servant leadership. Jesus did not teach His disciples to be doormats. Neither did He intend for the disciples to lord it over others. He called them to a new outlook on life that views power from a base of love rather than position. This leadership is symbolized best by the towel and wash basin rather than symbols of rank and wealth.

Art Criscoe states it well, "Jesus calls us to a different way of life. As Christians we have heard a different drummer and we are not to march in step with the world. We are called to a life of servant leadership."[2]

3

Models of Youth Ministry

A model represents an idea. A model airplane represents a real airplane. It allows a person to take a closer look by handling it, turning it, and looking at it from different angles. A model airplane is not the real thing but is a representation of the real thing.

Models of youth ministry allow us to take a look at some assumptions, activities, approaches, and philosophies of youth ministry. The models are never totally accurate, but they provide symbols that allow us to reflect on the various dimensions of youth ministry.

These models are not intended to be complete descriptions of any philosophies of youth ministry. They are simply snapshots of the visible evidence of several approaches to youth ministry that exist today.

Pied Piper

The Pied Piper is a youth minister who leads the parade, with youth following wherever the leader goes. Adults line the way, cheering him on, glad that the church has a youth minister the youth will love and follow. The Pied Piper may lead into some strange territories, but the youth and adults faithfully follow.

Peter Piper is the dynamic youth minister at a growing suburban church. He has obvious gifts in speaking and leading youth. He preaches to youth every week during a midweek youth meeting. The youth relate to him well, as evidenced by the ever larger numbers of youth who attend the youth group meetings. Peter plans and leads a lot of exciting youth activities. He usually speaks or entertains at these meetings and the youth love it. Parents and youth leaders are invited to help Peter by chaperoning and providing food for the youth activities.

The youth minister in this model tends to be an up-front, dynamic leader. He or she is like the Lone Ranger, operating freely and without regard of the other ministries of the church in planning youth activities. Adult leaders exist to help the Pied Piper carry out the youth ministry. Programs are usually planned and led by the youth minister. Activities tend to revolve around the Pied Piper youth minister.

This model has the advantage of being smooth and efficient, as long as the youth follow. A charismatic youth leader with a strong personality can usually draw large crowds of youth.

This model has three disadvantages. First, youth tend to idolize those with power and charisma. The highly visible youth minister may be busier pointing youth toward himself than toward Christ.

A second disadvantage has to do with the church's role in youth ministry. The Pied Piper, as the sole leader of the youth ministry, leaves little room for others to be involved. Parents, volunteer youth leaders, and other church members feel little responsibility or opportunity to be actively engaged in ministry with the youth.

Finally, when the Pied Piper marches off to another church, the youth ministry is left in confusion and disarray. If the ministry has been built around one person, others have not been equipped to carry on the work. Youth groups without a leader often go flat while they wait for a new Pied Piper.

Christian Guerrillas

This model of youth ministry is built around small core groups of highly dedicated youth who receive much attention from the youth minister. All youth are invited to be part of the core groups, but several receive special invitations because they have potential for leadership in the youth group.

Greg Guerrilla builds the youth ministry around small groups of highly committed, dedicated youth. These youth, mostly high-school age, meet during the week in homes of the members. Greg, along with several other handpicked youth leaders, spend a lot of time with these youth teaching, discipling, and modeling for them the various elements of the Christian life.

These small bands of Christian youth influence their peers by leading other groups themselves, speaking at youth meetings, and displaying their Christian life-style. Greg often speaks about spiritual warfare when all the youth group meets. Newcomers are urged to become more involved and become part of the small groups that meet at a different time during the week.

The Christian guerrillas model is aimed toward peer leadership. A few youth leaders pour time, energy, and attention into small groups of selected youth, who in turn influence the entire group with their attitudes and commitment. Parents and other youth leaders are involved only marginally.

One advantage of this model has to do with the hunger some youth feel for growth in spiritual areas. Adolescence is a time of searching and inquiry. Spiritual questions pose problems that cry out for answers. Some teenagers relate well to the intense discussions and challenges of small core groups.

Another advantage relates to the topics of study in this model. The core groups may deal seriously with topics of interest to the youth and provide a context for personal exploration in depth. The topic of spiritual warfare may, if handled appropriately, help many youth face temptations and live more consistently Christian life-styles.

This model has some distinct disadvantages. First, it tends to be exclusive rather than inclusive. The dedicated youth receive most of the attention, while youth on the fringe receive only token concern. Youth leaders who are leaders of the small core groups rank higher than those who serve in other areas of the church. Parents have little involvement in this model.

Second, youth should not be considered the primary channel for teaching and training. While youth can and do influence their peers in attitudes and behaviors, they do not perform well as teachers and group leaders for their peers over long periods. They need the continued support and presence of adult leaders with the groups they lead.

Finally, the youth minister in this model may resemble the Pied Piper if other youth leaders only serve in secondary roles. If all plans and activities originate with the general of the Christian guerrillas, then that person has also become the Pied Piper.

While it is true that Jesus spent large blocks of time with selected disciples, the concept must be adapted to youth ministry. Jesus was not dealing with adolescents but with adults. Also, He spent a great deal of time with many others—the 5,000 (Matt. 14; Luke 9), the seventy (Luke 10), the sick and outcasts (Matt. 19:2; Luke 9:6), Mary and Martha (John 12), and sinners and nonreligious people (Matt. 11:19).

Activities Director

The activities director has a busy calendar! The youth ministry is built around a series of exciting, youth-oriented activities designed to attract and entertain teenagers. The fact that some of the activities have little to do with Christian faith does not seem to be a problem.

Allison Activity is a dynamo of ideas. Projects, events, trips, banquets, games, socials, retreats, and youth seminars pour forth in a stream of creativity. She involves a lot of people in planning, promoting, and preparing for the events. The events attract a lot of teenagers, but many do not attend Bible study or the worship services of the church. Allison worries about making each event bigger, more exciting, and better attended than the last.

The activity director model is popular because it is easy to promote.

"There's always something going on for our youth!" Youth are promised more excitement and adventure at the next youth activity. Their lives may be permanently warped, they are warned, if they miss the next youth event. The advantage of this model grows out of the appeal of the activities to many youth who otherwise would not be interested in the church.

The disadvantages of this model are hard to deny but easy to ignore. With a lot of youth participating in activities, it may be hard to criticize the approach. But, the youth may be participating in a program that is superficial and shallow. If the activities are primarily for entertainment, the youth could be missing out on critical learning and direction in their spiritual growth.

The youth minister in this model can become a manager of a large youth social organization. Rather than serving as an authentic minister of the gospel, the activities director could be channeling too much energy and time into scheduling and conducting a series of disconnected, dated calendar events.

Big Happy Family

The big happy family is almost a nonyouth ministry. In this model the youth are integrated into the congregation in every facet of church life. A network of relationships includes youth in choir, worship, children's activities, church suppers, and ministry at every level.

Uncle Youthfriend is only one of the adults who meet with the youth at various times for fellowship and teaching. He teaches the youth group on Sunday mornings, but many other adults are considered friends by the teenagers. A typical worship service finds youth singing in the choir, leading a children's group in another room, playing the piano, serving as ushers, sitting with adults in the congregation, offering prayers, and reading the Bible at the pulpit. Adults shake hands, hug the youth, and linger to talk with youth after the service.

The youth are so integrated into the total life of the church, as both members and young leaders, that they rarely have activities only for them. In this model the youth often lead singing, preach sermons, and serve in many positions of leadership.

This model appears to have some desirable strengths. The youth feel loved and accepted. They sense ownership for their church and participate in most of the activities. They have a network of friends across the generations.

But, there are some disadvantages. First, youth who have not grown up in the church may not be easily accepted. Youth on the fringe may not be eager to participate at first.

Second, the youth ministry is hard to identify, and many youth will feel neglected, even among a crowd of friends. Youth have some developmental needs which the church should consider and address. Intergenerational activities are desirable, but youth also need some times for study and socializing with peers.

Junior Church

The junior church model also involves youth in many areas of church life. However, the youth operate on a separate layer from the adults.

Tammy Teamleader meets with elected representatives of the youth group at an annual planning retreat. They divide into teams to plan for youth involvement in worship, Bible study, mission activities, socials, sports, and ministry projects. The youth assume significant roles of leadership, and Tammy serves as a sponsor, enabler, and guide. The youth representatives return from their retreat with a calendar of youth activities that cover most areas of church life.

The youth conduct most of their own activities, just as the adults do. Since the youth often meet separately, there is not as much integration into the congregational life as in the big happy family model. The youth carry on a junior church that runs almost parallel to that of the congregation.

This model has some advantages to commend. It involves youth at a high level of leadership. Youth do not burn out as quickly, since they planned many of the projects. Relationships between the youth and the adults who serve with them can be close and rewarding.

But, there are some dangers. First, simply identifying selected areas and involving youth in leadership in those areas does not tap the richness of relationships in the total church family. Youth miss out on significant times of worship and growth by not being closely involved in corporate experiences.

A second danger arises when youth move out of the youth group. As they grow older, they should assume leadership and become involved with other adults, but they may tend to hang on to the friends in the junior church group or drop out of the adult circles when they grow too old for the youth group. Youth can be involved in the life and ministry of the body today as well as being trained as the leaders of tomorrow.

Equipper

The most promising model involves youth, parents, youth leaders, and church staff in a teamwork of shared ministry. This model considers youth as vital components of the body of Christ as well as objects of ministry. Youth are encouraged and equipped to participate in learning and service in significant ways.

Youth leaders are considered authentic ministers who are gifted and enabled to serve. The youth minister and other church staff see their ministry as equipping people to discover and use their spiritual gifts in a multitude of ways. Parents are included as vital links between home and church.

4

The Basics of Youth Ministry

Basic Definitions in Youth Ministry

Youth Ministry

Bob Taylor defines youth ministry as "enabling and mobilizing the gifts of many persons to touch, with the truths of the gospel, the lives of youth in every realm of their being."[3] This includes the sum total of all a church does with, for, and to youth. It includes the work done by church staff youth leaders as well as volunteer leaders of youth. It includes ministry with parents of youth.

Youth Minister

A youth minister is a minister of the gospel with specific responsibilities for leading the church's ministry to youth. He or she seeks to involve adult leaders of youth, parents of youth, other church staff, and youth themselves in sharing the church's ministry to youth. A youth minister may be serving in a combination role along with other responsibilities.

The youth minister is not a junior pastor or a director of youth activities. These imply only a portion of the responsibilities for youth ministry.

Youth Ministry Coordinator

A volunteer youth leader with responsibility for the overall youth ministry of a church is a youth ministry coordinator. This person may or may not be considered part of the church staff team.

Today's youth ministry faces an array of new challenges. Runaway chemical abuse, frightening diseases, a radically secularized society, declining moral values, and rapidly changing family structures are only a few of the issues confronting youth today. These issues call for a broad, deep, and theologically sound youth ministry. A youth minister who simply plans a series of social activities, exciting trips, and titillating discussions—no matter how appealing those may be—will fall short of adequate youth ministry.

Basic Concepts of Youth Ministry

An effective youth ministry will be built on some basic concepts. The following concepts represent the best in today's youth ministry, tried and proven in churches, large and small, across the country.

Every Church Has a Youth Ministry

A youth ministry cannot be judged by the number of fellowships and social events on the calendar. Some have mistakenly said: "We have nothing for our youth in this church. Let's call a youth minister and start a youth program."

Every church that has youth and is doing *anything* (a Sunday School class, or even youth in a worship service) is already doing some form of youth ministry. A better approach is to strengthen the work already being done, no matter how weak it may appear, and then build on this foundation by supporting it with social activities that add the sparkle to attract youth. Social events are strong outreach tools and strengthen a weakened group in need of life and vitality.

Youth leaders need encouragement and support. A wise youth minister will look for ways to equip and motivate adults who will touch the lives of youth in multiplied ways. Youth ministry is much bigger than parties, games, and fellowships. It includes everything done with, by, for, and to youth by a church.

Youth Ministry Is Not a Separate Program

A youth minister or a church does not have to start a youth program from scratch. By channeling the social and recreational activities through the church program organizations, youth ministry is linked to the ongoing work of the church. Sunday School departments and classes, church discipleship and missions education groups, and youth music groups receive adequate attention and promotion to make a balanced, effective youth ministry.

A youth minister who spends time sharing or strengthening a youth discipleship group and scheduling specialized discipleship training events related to the church's training program will accomplish more than simply leading a discipleship group of selected youth.

A youth minister who encourages youth Sunday School workers by meeting with them and providing training for them will develop a better Bible teaching program than one she leads on her own. The time spent in planning and leading one group can be better used equipping leaders who will reach multiplied numbers of youth for Sunday morning Bible study.

Youth Ministry Strikes a Balance in Two Important Areas

Reaching and teaching.—These two concerns should not be in competition. The Great Commission (Matt. 28:18-20) commands us to reach all we can and teach all we reach. Some youth leaders have mistakenly gone to extremes in one of these two directions. Events and strategies should be planned to reach and attract all the youth possible. Churches should make every effort to reach out to lost people and bring them to a saving relationship with Christ. However, we should never neglect the teaching ministry of the church.

Likewise we should plan to make our teaching of the highest quality possible. Creative teaching methods, proper planning, and adequate learning environment should always be priorities. But youth who have never been in church before will not know how to relate to some church routines. We must prepare to teach people at their level of understanding.

Integrating and separating.—Youth must see themselves as related to the total work of the church. Youth ministry must be more than a satellite group barely linked to the church. Youth activities should be coordinated with the total church calendar to avoid overlaps and conflicts.

However, youth are in a critical stage of life and need specialized attention from a church. A seventh-grade girl is different from her seventy-year-old grandmother. A twelfth-grade boy faces different needs from his middle-aged father.

Many churches use at least four age divisions—preschool, children, youth, and adult. Churches must work to meet the needs of each of these groups and still help them be integrated into the total work of the church. A balance between integration into the whole church family and separation into age groups is a vital concern of youth ministry.

Youth Ministry Is a Shared Ministry

Today's youth ministry demands more than a lone ranger leader for the youth group. Even the smallest youth groups have a variety of ministry needs. Ephesians 4 teaches that God has gifted the saints (all Christians) for the work of ministry. The stereotype of the up-front, charismatic, youthful leader who plays a guitar, leads exciting games, and holds a group spellbound with a lecture is a weak model for youth ministry. Youth also need the gifts of prayer, mercy, hospitality, exhortation, teaching, and service along with the more visible gifts.

The arena of youth ministry includes the work done by the youth minister and other church staff, volunteer leaders of youth, parents of youth, and youth themselves. The following illustration symbolizes the relationships that make up a youth minister's work.

Youth Ministry Relationships

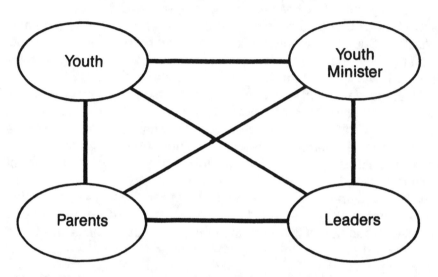

Youth ministry means more than relating well to teenagers. A youth minister must also relate well to adults who in turn relate to youth. In fact, about two-thirds of a youth minister's functions and energies must be spent in planning for and working with adults who impact the lives of teenagers. This calls for maturity and skills in relating well to adult leaders of youth and parents of youth.

Youth Ministry Touches All Aspects of a Youth's Life

The spiritual part of life cannot be separated from other aspects of life. Physical, mental, social, and emotional development has a great deal to do with spiritual development. Youth leaders must be as concerned with a youth's life on Saturday night as they are with that same youth on Sunday morning.

The family situation, grades at school, physical development, self-image, and peer groups are vital elements of a youth's life. God is actively interested in these areas of life, and youth leaders should be also. This requires us to move out from the walls of the church and become acquainted with the world of our youth. Youth leaders cannot hope to relate to youth if they only see them at church. Ball games, after-school hangouts, homes of youth, and places they work are the locations for meeting youth in their own territory. By seeing youth in these places and allowing youth to see them there, youth leaders earn the right to be heard in youth groups at church.

Youth Ministry Belongs to the Church

Who owns the youth ministry of your church? The youth minister? The deacons or pastor? The youth? The youth leaders or parents? Ultimately Jesus Christ is the owner of the church and all it does. The day-to-day stewardship of youth ministry belongs to the church. Youth ministers are servants of the church charged with the responsibility to lead the church in doing *the church's* youth ministry. It does not belong to any one individual, especially the youth minister. If so, the youth ministry will almost disappear when the youth minister moves on to another church. This roller-coaster effect is all too familiar to those churches with a youth ministry built around one person.

Churches must realize the awesome responsibility of ministering with today's youth and be willing to supply the people and resources to do so. Youth ministers must realize the responsibility they have for involving the total church—adult youth leaders, parents, youth, and other staff—in ministering to youth in this critical time of life.

Two Philosophies of Youth Ministry [4]

Two approaches to youth ministry are seen in churches today, representing two different philosophies. One of these, the activity-based youth program, is less appropriate than the ministry-based approach to youth ministry.

The *activity-based approach* usually centers around a youth minister who leads a busy schedule of youth activities. These activities might include social activities as well as spiritual growth times. The key distinctive, however, is the relationship to the total life and work of the church. The following illustration represents an activity-based youth program.

The left half of the illustration represents the scope of the ongoing work of the church through the church program organizations. The right half represents a youth program led by and built around the youth minister (often called a youth director). This kind of ministry usually begins with an abundance of social and recreational activities such as 1parties, games, fellowships, trips, sports, and so forth. Then, in order to keep a spiritual balance, Bible studies, discipleship groups, mission trips, and concerts are added.

The weakness of this approach lies in the relationship of these activities—both social and spiritual—to the ongoing work of the church. Most of the social activities are simply a series of projects and events

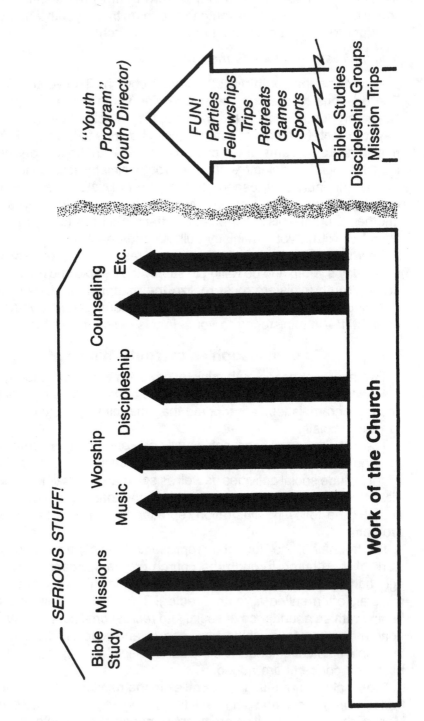

Activity-Based Approach

"Youth Program" (Youth Director)

FUN!
Parties
Fellowships
Trips
Retreats
Games
Sports

Bible Studies
Discipleship Groups
Mission Trips

SERIOUS STUFF!

Bible Study
Missions
Music
Worship
Discipleship
Counseling
Etc.

Work of the Church

Ministry-Based Approach

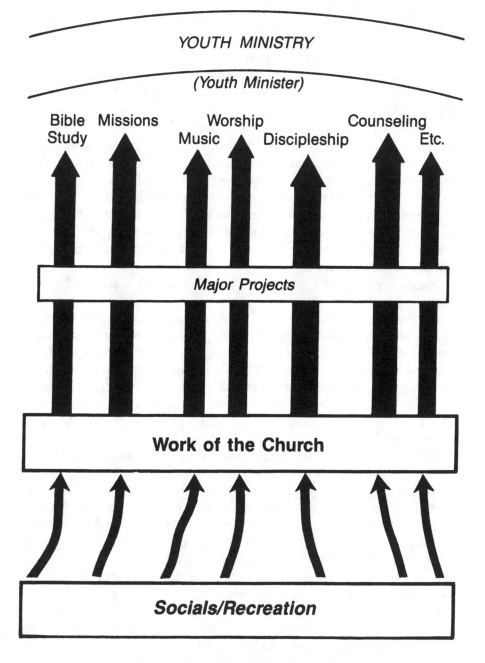

*Major Projects could include Youth Camp,
Youth-Led Revivals, Concerts, etc.*

with little or no relationship to other programs that involve youth. This creates a dividing wall between the "fun activities" sponsored by the youth minister, and the activities that seem "boring," such as Bible study and discipleship classes.

Even the spiritual growth activities have little relationship to other-youth programs. Bible study is not related to Sunday School; the discipleship groups have no connection to church-sponsored discipleship training; and the mission trips are planned and led by the youth minister with no input or involvement from the church mission organizations. A spirit of competition and duplication develops, and eventually the youth program organizations suffer. Youth Sunday School becomes less appealing when compared to the "indepth" Bible study led by the youth minister at the pizza restaurant on Saturday night. The church mission organization cannot compete with the mission trip to Disney World. The church-planned discipleship groups struggle because of less attention from the youth minister who is busy leading his own discipleship course.

A more appropriate philosophy of youth ministry is pictured in the following illustration.

This *ministry-based approach* is built around a team of ministering leaders and is channeled primarily through the youth church organizations. Notice the similarities with the activity-based approach. Many social-recreational activities and spiritual growth times remain. However, these are closely related to the youth program organizations. Parties, games, fellowships, trips, and other activities are planned and conducted whenever feasible by the youth program organizations of the church.

Spiritual growth activities reside in the youth program organizations. Bible study is always related in some way to Sunday School. This includes Sunday morning, weekday, Wednesday night, and other special Bible study events. Discipleship training is vitally linked to the discipleship, doctrinal, and ethical training available through the church's ongoing program. Youth receive missions education and involvement around the year, not just once a year on a trip, because the church missions education groups receive the encouragement and support needed to have a vital youth missions education program.

Recreation supports the church program organizations. Whenever possible, recreational events are sponsored, planned, and conducted by the youth program organizations. Of course, some events cut across program lines (an all-youth banquet or a youth-adult partnership revival), but even these events can be broken up and portions assigned to different groups for planning and promotion. This ensures a balance between the fun and the spiritual by linking the two together.

Evangelism saturates the work of the youth program organizations. Each organization carries a portion of the emphasis on evangelism. Sunday School takes the lead in outreach and evangelistic Bible study. The church discipleship program equips youth in witness training and discipleship. The missions education groups and youth music groups seek to involve youth in evangelism at home and around the world.

The ministry-based approach requires a team of leaders rather than the lone ranger approach of the activity-based youth program. Youth ministry is too big for one person working alone. It must be integrated with the total work of other leaders who work with youth in the church, parents of youth, other church staff members, and youth themselves.

Moving Toward a Ministry Base

In the first church I served as a youth minister, I worked almost totally with the youth. There were a few adults who volunteered to help with youth fellowships and banquets, but I did most of the planning and promotion. I also did most of the work.

I would enlist some of the youth to help brainstorm ideas for the next banquet, fellowship, or party. Then we would ask a few adults to help chaperon. There was no relationship to anything else the youth were doing in the church.

One Sunday I dropped by the departments where the youth were having Bible study. I realized I did not know any of the adults working with those youth. I did not know what they did on Sunday morning, how they conducted the Bible studies, or how they related to the youth in their groups outside of Sunday morning.

I knew only a little about parents and family members of the youth in my group. When I talked with the pastor about this, I discovered that the church had always looked upon youth ministry as the extracurricular activities that went along with the study, ministry, and worship of the rest of the church. Youth ministry was simply planning the fun element while others ministered in serious ways.

Many youth ministers find this same attitude in churches across the country. Churches and church leaders sincerely want to appeal to youth and keep them involved in the life of their church. They do this by scheduling a series of youth-oriented social and recreational activities but never move beyond that. The activities are never integrated into the ministry of the church. The youth ministry remains a program separate from the life and work of the church.

How does a youth minister change this attitude? How does one move from an activity-based program to a ministry-based approach to youth ministry? Here are some practical suggestions. These work over a period of time, but they are not a formula for instant success. The process usually takes more than a year to accomplish.

Discuss Philosophy and Approaches to Youth Ministry During the Interview Process

While you visit with a search committee or pastor, ask about the church's approach to youth ministry. Ask questions such as: How would you describe the ideal youth minister? What kind of youth minister are you seeking? What do you see as the youth minister's role in the church? This is a good time to discuss different approaches to youth ministry and share your views on the subject.

Schedule a Meeting with Youth Leaders

Meet with all youth leaders (Sunday School workers, discipleship leaders, missions education leaders, music leaders, coaches, sponsors, and anyone else who works with youth in any capacity) as soon as possible after beginning your new position. Discuss the ideas of a shared ministry approach to youth ministry. Help them see their work as a vital part of the total youth ministry of the church. Help them see you as a coleader and facilitator of their ministry, not the leader of a separate approach to youth ministry.

Schedule a Meeting with Parents

Meet with all parents of teenagers in the church soon after you begin your ministry. Become acquainted with them and help them become acquainted with other parents of teenagers. Find out what they think about the past, present, and future of the youth ministry in the church. Ask such questions as: What has the church done with youth in the past that you really like? What would you like to see changed? What would you like to see happen in your teenagers' lives by the time they graduate from high school?

Write all these responses on a large chalkboard or on newsprint so that they can see the magnitude of youth ministry. Then use these responses to illustrate the need for many adults—parents, volunteer leaders, church staff, and the youth minister—working together to accomplish the goals for the church's youth ministry. Assure the parents of your support for them and desire for their support of the youth ministry. Allow parents to give input into the direction of the church's youth ministry.

Schedule a Discussion Time for the Youth

This is often one of the first things youth ministers do when they begin a new ministry. The get-acquainted meetings with youth are important to establish relationships and begin building a sense of unity and direction for the youth group. The meetings with parents and youth leaders are equally important.

Ask the youth for their ideas about the direction of youth ministry in their church. Ask similar questions to those used with the parents. Use this time to build an attitude of teamwork in which youth are involved *with* the ministry and are not just *objects* of ministry.

Channel the Planning for Youth Activities
Through the Church Program Organizations

Involve the volunteer youth leaders in planning and conducting youth activities. Help them enlist youth to plan and conduct the activities for their groups. Offer resources, ideas, and funds to carry out the activities. A Sunday School worker who plans a fellowship for the youth group, involves the youth in the planning process, and is visible at the activity will build relationships that will strengthen the overall ministry of the church. That leader will begin to see herself as a true leader in the youth ministry. Youth will begin to sense ownership for the church's ministry with teenagers and will become more involved in other facets of spiritual growth.

Provide money for the different groups to carry out social and recreational activities for their groups. Sunday School classes, discipleship groups, mission groups, and music groups can all benefit from being involved in the planning process.

Delegate Responsibilities When Planning Large Projects

Some activities are too large to be handled by one group of youth and leaders. Youth camp, a large mission trip, youth-led revivals, and even a major social event require planning and work by many people. Enlist leaders and youth from all the church program organizations to take responsibilities for a portion of the work.

When possible, assign part of the work that relates to their program. For example, Bible study during youth camp could be planned by leaders and youth from the Sunday School groups. Follow up for new Christians during a youth-led revival could be coordinated by discipleship groups. Music for a youth banquet could be planned by those who work with youth music groups in the church.

Involve Parents in Youth Ministry

Seek the input of parents of teenagers concerning the church's youth ministry. Parents have hopes and dreams for their teenagers and often feel neglected and ignored by youth leaders in the church.

Feelings of frustration may result in negative attitudes and lack of support for the youth ministry if parents are not involved.

Schedule regular meetings for parental input, questions, and discussion about the youth ministry. Meetings with parents before major youth events (youth camp, trips, and so forth) are good, but most parents want to know more than what time the bus leaves and how much the event costs.

Parents may be enlisted to sponsor activities and lead different groups if they have a good relationship with their own teenager. Make sure the parents will not smother their son or daughter with supervision during the process. It may be better for some parents to work with an age group different from their own teenager.

Keep the Pastor and Staff Informed

Meet regularly with the pastor and staff for coordination, information, and staff planning. Share calendar plans, goals, and your vision for the church's youth ministry. Overwhelm the pastor with information when beginning a new ministry. It is better to overinform than to keep the pastor in the dark. Questions that arise about the youth ministry can be handled better when the pastor and staff know the full story about procedures and approaches.

Be Patient

Moving from an activity-based youth ministry to a ministry-based approach is a long process. It will not happen overnight, and there may be some resistance along the way. People may not understand what is happening or where the youth ministry is headed. They may not understand the role of the youth minister. Some may think the youth minister is simply trying to get out of work. Youth may fear that youth activities will cease. In fact, more youth activities usually take place as youth leaders across the church begin planning and leading activities for their groups.

The youth minister might fear losing touch with youth. As more adults become involved with the youth, will that mean the youth minister is simply an administrative figure head? Most of the time, the youth minister is relieved from mundane responsibilities and allowed more time for one-to-one relationships with youth. As more adults are equipped to do ministry with youth, the youth minister can move among the youth group and spend more time with those who need more personal attention.

5

Church Programs

A New Testament church worships God, proclaims the good news of Christ, educates and nurtures persons, and ministers to the world. These functions make up the primary stack poles of the life and work of the people of God in carrying out the Great Commission.

To perform these functions, we must identify specific tasks to be done on a regular basis. These tasks may be done by large or small groups. Sometimes they are done by people of all ages, while other tasks are done only by selected groups. Some tasks are basic concerns, fundamental to the life and work of the church. Other tasks are more supportive in nature. Still other tasks are emphases that need to be addressed in various ways.

These tasks can be formed into logical groupings that are called programs. Sometimes the word *program* is used to mean an activity, an event, or a plan to do some job. Programs often have negative images as being cold and impersonal. Some people avoid talking about programs and prefer to focus on people instead. This is a valid concern, but it misses the intention of church programs.

Church programs are to involve people in the church work. They are groupings of specific tasks that move toward performance of the functions and accomplishment of the mission of the church. A church program is not just an activity or event. It is the way a church organizes itself to worship, witness and proclaim, educate and nurture, and minister to people. Church tasks are grouped into three types of programs: basic programs, service programs, and emphasis programs.

Basic programs are groupings of tasks that are basic, continuing, and of primary concern to the church work. They seek to involve people of all ages in regular, weekly meetings and in special, short-term events. Basic programs consist of the Bible teaching, discipleship, music, missions education, and pastoral ministry tasks of the church.

Service programs are groupings of tasks, supportive in nature, that seek to serve the basic program organizations of the church. They are organized but may not involve all people in regular, ongoing meetings.

Service programs consist of such things as the recreational, media library, and administrative tasks of the church.

Emphasis programs are groupings of tasks or continuing concerns that are vital to the church life and work. However, due to the nature of these concerns, they do not occur in regular meetings with structured groups. Emphasis programs are usually channeled through the work of the basic programs. Emphasis concerns consist of the church tasks related to evangelism, family ministry, stewardship, church planting, vocational guidance, and the church work on college campuses.

For the purposes of this discussion, we will look closer at the specific church tasks related to the basic programs that involve youth. The youth program organizations include the Bible teaching, discipleship, music, and missions education program organizations.

Bible Teaching Program Tasks

The Bible teaching program, often called Sunday School, is the primary Bible teaching, ministry, and outreach arm of a church. This program involves youth in purposeful Bible study and outreach. The church tasks for this program include:

1. Reach youth for Bible study.
2. Teach youth the Bible.
3. Witness to youth and lead them into church membership.
4. Minister to youth members and nonmembers.
5. Lead youth to worship (both corporately and privately).
6. Interpret and undergird the work of the church and denomination.

Discipleship Program Tasks

The discipleship program is the primary discipling arm of the church. This is the key avenue for training youth in Christian theology and ethics, disciplines of the Christian faith, leadership, and churchmanship. Although youth will be exposed to theology and discipleship at other times in church groups, this is the opportunity for purposeful learning and application of these disciplines. The church tasks related to this program include:

1. Reach youth for discipleship.
2. Orient new Christians and church members for responsible church membership.
3. Equip youth for discipleship and personal ministry.
4. Teach youth Christian theology and doctrine, Christian ethics, Christian history, and other topics related to Christian churchmanship.
5. Train youth in leadership.
6. Interpret and undergird the work of the church and denomination.

Missions Education Program Tasks

Missions education and action is central to the church life and work. This is the primary means for involving youth in reaching beyond the walls of the church to pray for, support, and be actively engaged in missions. Since ministry action is Christian service to church members (an activity of the Bible teaching program), missions action is Christian service beyond the walls of the church to those persons who are not church members. Through these experiences youth most often hear and respond to the call for vocational Christian service in missions.

Some churches have separate missions groups for men and women, while others work through coeducational groupings. All groups seek to involve youth in missions. Church tasks related to the missions education programs include:

1. Teach missions.
2. Engage in mission actions and personal witnessing.
3. Support missions through prayer, offerings, personal ministries for missionaries, emphasizing the need to be involved in missions, and volunteer mission experiences.
4. Develop personal ministries related to missions.
5. Interpret and undergird the work of the church and denomination.

Music Program Tasks

Music is the soul of a church. Youth can learn to express their faith through a variety of musical experiences. Music provides a context for learning about and involvement in worship. Many youth have talents and gifts that can be developed through musical involvement. Church tasks related to the music program include:

1. Provide musical experiences for the congregational worship experience.
2. Provide church music education.
3. Lead youth to witness and minister through music.
4. Assist church programs in providing training in music skills and consultation about music equipment.
5. Interpret and undergird the work of the church and denomination.

The Role of Recreation and Evangelism

Youth ministry is more than fun and games, a flurry of social activities, and a busy calendar of recreational events. It is also more than intense study experiences and deeply serious training and discipling groups. Somewhere between these two experiences is a blend of appealing, wholesome approaches that attract and involve youth in ways that point them toward Christ and help them grow spiritually.

Recreation adds the spice to youth ministry. Recreation opens up doors for comfortable social relationships between youth, youth workers, and parents of youth. Recreation activities should be channeled through the ongoing church program organizations whenever possible. However, even the major youth activities, or parts of them, planned directly by the youth minister can be planned and conducted by the youth and leaders in the program organizations.

Evangelism should saturate all areas of youth ministry. Each of the programs has church tasks related to witnessing and outreach. Jesus demonstrated models of evangelism that included the full scope of relational, personal, and mass evangelism. Evangelism can be a vital part of youth ministry through the work of the church programs in social activities, witness training experiences, and evangelism events.

The Role of the Youth Minister in the Program Organizations

A glance at the church tasks mentioned above reveals a balanced approach to youth ministry. A church that is doing all those tasks is moving toward accomplishing its mission in a purposeful way.

But how does youth ministry relate to the work of the church program organizations? *The easiest way to answer this question is to see youth ministry as the sum total of all the church does with, for, and to youth.* This includes all the work done by the program organizations and all the relationships of youth and other persons in the church. Youth ministry is not a separate program that duplicates or competes with the work done by the different groups in the church.

The best relationship of youth ministry to the church program organizations is one of mutual support and encouragement. Youth ministry resides in the program organizations. The program organizations, supported by recreation and saturated with evangelism, are the channels of ministry for youth ministry in the church.

A youth minister who encourages and strengthens the work done by the Bible teaching program will have a more complete and solid Bible teaching approach to youth ministry. A youth minister who builds upon the work done by the discipleship and missions training programs seeks to enhance the discipling and missions emphasis of these groups and plans ways to expand their work will multiply the overall effectiveness of youth ministry. A youth minister who views the music ministry as an ally rather than a competitor will reap the benefits of a comprehensive, well-balanced youth ministry.

6

A Network of Relationships

We live in a fragmented world. Too often people are separated into groups for the convenience of some program, marketing approach, or activity. We are identified by race, gender, zip codes, age, income, size of house, number of cars in the driveway, place of business, credit rating, and other factors. The church is even guilty at some points.

We tend to segregate groups for programming and ministry. We group people according to age for educational programs and interest activities. We plan special activities for preschoolers, married adults, single adults, youth, children, men, women, and senior adults. We offer seminars for senior adults, exercise classes for women, crafts for children, prayer breakfasts for men, and mission projects for youth.

These are worthy experiences, but they all tend to keep people apart. Youth can learn from adults of all ages. A hug or handshake from a senior adult can mean as much as having a good time at a retreat. A youth who longs for attention will respond to someone of any age who shows love and concern.

Youth ministry should build bridges across the generations. A youth minister who spends time only with youth misses out on valuable opportunities for growth and assistance in ministry that can come from all of God's people.

Youth ministers must relate well to parents of youth. Parents are the strongest influence on their teenagers.[5] If we hope to influence youth toward Christ, we must influence the homes of youth. Youth ministers must inform parents of youth activities, equip parents for their parenting roles, and support parents in the task of parenting their teenagers.

Youth leaders are important because of the relationships they have with youth on a regular basis. Adults who teach, lead, counsel, sponsor youth activities, coach, and love teenagers should be equipped and enabled to do youth ministry. They can visit with youth during the week and see them at church and school functions. Good relationships between the youth minister and volunteer youth leaders will multiply the ministry with youth.

Youth are important members of the church family. They need the growth and joy that comes from mutual involvement in the larger congregational experiences. A youth group that is only an appendix to the life of the church family is missing the wealth of relationships that comes from the whole family of God. By seeing the whole growth cycle and ways God works with people of all ages, youth can learn more about the constant, all-encompassing love and concern of God. Youth ministry should be ministry *with* youth and not just *for* or *to* youth.

A youth minister can assure these relationships by viewing youth ministry in thirds. A third of the youth ministry with parents, a third with youth leaders, and a third with youth will point the ministry toward balance of peer and intergenerational activities. This will involve more people in youth ministry, providing a more balanced approach.

Youth Ministry Time Chart

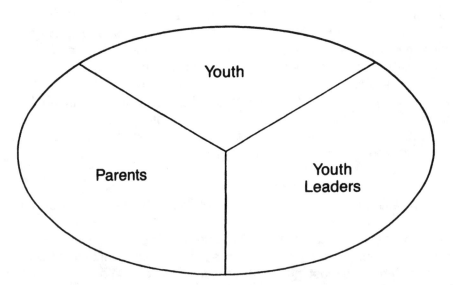

The time chart above shows the philosophy of youth ministry built around these three relationships. Spending time in each area assures a comprehensive strategy of ministry. The time does not have to be spent directly with parents or leaders. But this may include time spent planning for ministry, training, and support of each of these groups. Time spent planning ways to strengthen the work done by youth leaders as they teach in the various groups is time well spent. Time spent planning ways to strengthen homes of youth or minister to their parents will reap benefits beyond time spent planning another fellowship.

Youth ministry must also be correlated with other ministries through the work of the church staff. The youth minister is first and foremost a *minister* rather than a director of youth activities. This calls for a desire to work alongside other staff members to avoid competition, petty jealousies, and overemphasis in some areas of church work.

The church may not have all the programs listed in this chapter. There may be other groups doing the work of ministry in your church. All educational, missions, discipling, and music program organizations can have an impact on the youth in their groups.

The youth ministry has a responsibility for coordinating the work done by every group that touches the lives of youth in the church. This coordination does not imply control over the groups . Rather, it calls for the youth minister to facilitate and support the work done by the organization, be aware of plans and special activities, be involved in enlisting and equipping leaders, and seek ways to improve the contribution that group makes to the overall youth ministry of the church. A wise youth minister will look for ways to share leadership with many adults who in turn will touch the lives of youth.

Part 2
Youth Ministry with Adult Leaders

7

Adult Leaders of Youth

The Role of Adult Leaders

Effective youth ministry requires a team of dedicated, committed adults who can minister to youth and involve them in a journey of Christian discipleship. Youth need to know adults of all ages so they can see Christianity in action. Adult leaders model what faith means in everyday life. Youth benefit from the teaching, influence, and love of adults who assist them in celebrating the good news of Jesus Christ.

Ephesians sounds a clear message for youth ministers and other church staff. Those who have been called to ministry have been given gifts, not for doing all the work of ministry, but for "the equipping of the saints for the work of service, to the building up of the body of Christ" (Eph. 4:12). We should be busy mobilizing people to touch the lives of youth for Christ.

Ephesians mentions several spiritual gifts that can be used in spiritual leadership. God gives gifts to accomplish His will. God does not call people into service and then abandon them. Rather, He gifts people with potential for service. If God intends for something to happen, He supplies the power to bring it about through the spiritual gifts He gives to all Christians. It is the task of the youth minister to help people discover their spiritual gifts and find places of expression for those gifts.

Many adults want to serve in youth ministry but hesitate to volunteer because they do not feel adequate, trained, or equipped to lead youth. Youth ministers may hesitate to enlist adults because of a desire to control the youth ministry. Still others may feel that involving volunteer leaders makes it appear the youth minister cannot handle the job alone.

Let's face it—youth ministry is a big job! It is time-consuming, challenging, and exhausting work. It calls for the talents and energies of a team of leaders. Pastors need to be involved in youth ministry by their support and encouragement from the pulpit and their presence at youth events. Parents need to be involved in youth ministry by being aware and informed of youth ministry goals and activities. Parents should have opportunities to serve as chaperons and give input to the direction of youth ministry. Other adults can lead teenagers toward a growing maturity in faith. Adolescents need more than religious instruction; they need to see Christian faith in the warmth of adults who care deeply for them.

Equipping Adult Leaders

Today's youth ministry is much broader than the old style of providing fellowship activities after church on Sunday night. The needs of adolescents and their families in the latter part of the twentieth century are staggering. A "Coke and a joke" might have kept young people entertained in some bygone era, although that approach never was spiritually adequate. Youth ministry must touch the lives of youth in all areas: social, emotional, physical, mental, and spiritual.

Drug abuse, alcoholism, sexual pressures, suicide, sexually transmitted diseases, family breakdown, and an increasingly secular society are just a few of the issues facing youth today. Guiding youth in their spiritual decisions and growth is a tremendous challenge for today's youth leader.

Leading a youth group also calls for multiple gifts and energies. Teachers for Sunday School classes, leaders for discipleship and missions education groups, coaches, sponsors for youth trips, and counselors for camps and retreats must be found and trained.

The youth minister who tries to do all this alone has a severe handicap. It is like trying to accomplish the mission of the church with both hands and feet tied. In fact, 1 Corinthians 12:12-27 gives a picture of the church as a body with the members like different parts of the body. All the parts are important, and all the parts need to be equipped for ministry.

Why Do Adults Volunteer to Serve in Youth Ministry?

Adults volunteer to lead in youth ministry for a variety of reasons. Some reasons are appropriate, while other motives are less than ideal. The Holy Spirit gives gifts for the work of ministry, but those gifts may be abused in the midst of emotions, clashing personalities, and misguided priorities. Understanding why youth leaders serve will aid youth ministers in their equipping ministry.

Many youth leaders serve out of a sense of calling and a desire to serve God and their brothers and sisters in Christ. God calls volunteers into youth ministry as surely as He calls those who serve Him in paid positions.

Others serve out of a desire for self-fulfillment. There is a certain level of recognition from youth and other adult church members for those who teach classes, sponsor trips, and counsel youth. Some adults need the strokes and attention that come from being with younger people and being seen as a leader. Status and approval are poor substitutes for the sense of calling that comes from God.

Others serve out of a sense of guilt. A person may feel that he has a debt to pay for past sins. He may feel that his adolescent years were wasted and that working with youth is a way to "pay back" for those misspent years. Still others serve because no one else will, and they feel the church needs to provide leadership for their youth. They serve out of duty and responsibility rather than as grateful response to God's leadership in their lives.

A youth minister has the responsibility of equipping the saints for ministry, regardless of the reason for their service. There is room for counseling those who are serving for the wrong reason. Certainly this should be considered in enlisting any future youth leaders. However, the youth minister must often patiently serve with those who are still searching for God's leadership in how they serve Him.

Finding Leaders—Experienced youth ministers always look for potential youth leaders. But finding adults who will volunteer to teach, lead, coach, and counsel with teenagers is sometimes difficult. Here are some suggestions for locating adults for potential leadership positions:

1. *Scan the rolls of adult Bible study groups.*—Adults who are members of Sunday School classes are not serving in other positions of leadership during that time. They could be teachers for youth groups during Sunday School.

2. *Look at the list of parents of youth.*—Parents often want to be involved with their teenagers but don't know how to get started. Use caution in assigning a parent to work with a son or daughter. Sometimes it works, but some parents just cannot change their parental role when in a group with their teenager.

3. *Look for adults who have worked with youth previously.*—Ask other church staff members, youth leaders, and members of the church.

4. *Consider college or seminary students.*—If you are near a college or seminary you might have students who are willing to serve in youth leadership positions. Students often work best in short-term positions (counselors at camps and retreats, sponsors for activities, leaders for special studies, and so forth). Be aware that students often want to go home during semester breaks and school holidays, since this may be a hardship on other leaders in the youth group.

5. *Consider senior adults.*—Some of the best youth leaders I have

known were senior adults. They have time to give to youth activities and often enjoy working with teenagers. Senior adults with a positive outlook on life can bring joy and excitement to youth and provide a beautiful model of Christian faith in a different generation from adolescents.

Enlisting Leaders—Finding adults who can be potential leaders is not an impossible task. But enlisting them to serve may be more of a challenge. I have found this process to work effectively in enlisting adults:[1]

1. *Approach with the process with prayer.*—Prayer should saturate all that we do in ministry. This does not mean that we ask God to please help fill a line on our nominating committee report.

There is a theological principle involved. The Bible teaches that God gives gifts to accomplish His will (1 Cor. 12:4-11). If He desires for a task to be accomplished, a class to be taught, or a group to be led, then God has already given the gifts to accomplish those tasks. It is the minister's responsibility to help people discover their spiritual gifts and put those gifts into ministry. It is not our task to pressure, persuade, or cajole people to accept a leadership role. Through prayer we are led to those people who are best gifted to do the work of youth ministry.

2. *Develop an awareness of potential leaders.*—Make a list of those adults who could become youth leaders. Look around at church services, socials, choir rehearsals, and other activities. Be alert for adults who could become youth leaders. Do not rule out any age group but be open to the possibility of using young, median, and senior adults. Begin praying for those on your list.

3. *Help people understand adolescents.*—Many adults fear teenagers because of negative images they receive from the media. News reports of gangs, juvenile delinquency, drug and sexual abuse, and rebellion is enough to scare anyone. Exploitation of teenagers through movies and other media paints a grim picture of adolescent life. Many adults view teenagers as mutant creatures ready to devour anyone unfortunate enough to be in the same room with them.

Help ease fears by showing teenagers in a better light. Let youth take part in worship times, when the congregation can see a more positive image. Ask adults to drive youth from church to a youth fellowship. Invite adults to help serve during snack suppers on Sunday nights, prepare food for a youth activity, or drive a car during youth outreach activities. Give adults contact with youth during informal, positive activities.

4. *Plant seeds with potential leaders.*—Mention that sometime in the future a person could become a good youth leader. Ask if a person

has ever thought about serving in youth ministry. Ask if the person has worked with youth before. Affirm the gifts or talents that appear to be good qualities of youth leaders.

5. *Involve potential leaders in a structured situation.*—Let the potential worker observe a structured teaching-learning group. Adults may fear that youth will ask deep theological questions. Most youth leaders would welcome any kind of questions from their group! The potential leader will get a better feel for the actual process of teaching and learning with youth. They can discover that it is all right not to know all the answers. The best response is usually to admit you do not know the answer and search for an answer with the youth.

6. *Invite the person to youth leader training.*—It is normally easier to enlist someone to be equipped to lead than it is to enlist them for immediate responsibilities. Those who have never worked with youth might hesitate because they feel inadequate.

The enlisting method is important. Make an appointment to talk with the person. Go to the home, meet for a meal, or invite him or her to your office. Assure the person that you have prayed about the invitation. Describe the training and the possibilities of future service in youth leadership.

When enlisting someone to serve in a specific position of youth leadership, follow a similar method. However, spell out the responsibilities, the expectations of the church, how you and other youth leaders will relate to them, and the joys and challenges of the job. People usually appreciate knowing in advance what the job is like.

Give the candidate some time to ask questions and consider the offer. Do not push for an immediate answer. Instead, encourage the person to pray about the offer and give an answer in a short while. It is helpful to set a date for another discussion when the person can give a definite answer and accept or reject the invitation.

Youth Leader Training

Youth leaders need training at several levels. They need training in basic Christian leadership, potential youth leader training, program organization training, and specific job training. The following diagram illustrates these areas of youth leadership training.[2]

Areas of Youth Leadership Training

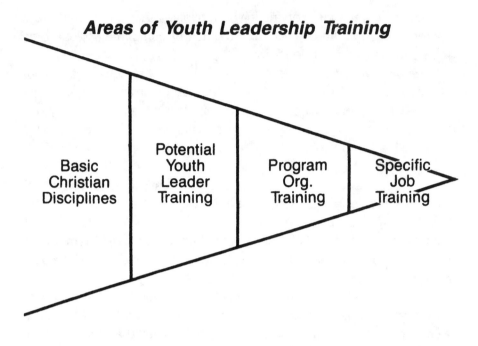

Basic Christian Leadership Training—This is the basic orientation and follow-up for new Christians. It also includes the training in disciplines of the Christian life that facilitates growth in Christian maturity. This training includes content areas such as understanding of salvation, forgiveness, prayer, Bible study, witnessing, living under the guidance and power of the Holy Spirit, and so forth. This training can be covered in informal discipleship relationships with another Christian, Bible study classes, structured discipleship and evangelism groups, and other regular and short-term classes

Potential Youth Leader Training—This includes study and growth in Christian leadership, understanding of adolescence, youth ministry methods and processes, and an overview of the opportunities of service in youth ministry. A typical thirteen-week (three- month) course could include:

• Potential Leadership Training (six sessions)—Training and study in biblical models of leadership, styles of leadership, what youth leaders do, discovery of spiritual gifts and how to use them in youth leadership, and how to continue growing spiritually.

• Basic Youth Leadership Training (six sessions)—Basic skills in teaching methods, how to handle discipline, planning youth Bible study sessions, understanding adolescence, and skills in building relationships with adolescents.

• Overview of Youth Ministry (one session)—A survey of basic principles of youth ministry and the relationship to church program organizations. This would inform potential leaders about possible opportunities for service in youth ministry.

Program Organization Training—A person who wants to serve in any program organization needs assistance with understanding the organizations in the church, using printed curriculum materials, understanding job descriptions, and building relationships with youth and involving them in the tasks of the program organization.

Specific Job Training—Within each program organization there are specific jobs to be done. People need to know what is expected and how to accomplish their jobs. A teacher in Sunday School, leader of a discipleship group, pianist for a youth music group, or counselor for a youth mission group all need some orientation. This training may be short and handled in a one-on-one meeting, but it is still important.

The sad truth is that much of our training is done only at this level. We often ignored training people in the foundations of youth ministry. That is one reason why so many youth leaders crash and burn after a few short months of service. Basic skills and understandings in youth ministry may have been ignored or overlooked.

Involving Parents in Ministry

Parents have a built-in understanding of many of the concerns and interests of teenagers. Contrary to the stereotypes, parents are not always "in the dark" about the world of teenagers. They observe the clothes teenagers wear, the music they listen to, and the conversations between their teenager and her friends. They are aware of physical growth, mood swings, and anxiety about the first date. Although parents may not completely understand their teens and may not always get along with them, their awareness of adolescent development can be useful in youth ministry.

Some of the best youth leaders I have known were parents of teenagers in the youth group. (We won't talk about the ones who didn't work out too well.) Sunday School teachers, discipleship group leaders, softball coaches, and youth camp counselors have all come from the ranks of parents. Parents can be assets to youth ministry by serving in leadership positions or helping in a variety of ways.

Some precautions will help in the enlisting process. First, the parents must be able to "let go" of their own teenager if they are to be effective workers. One mother was a counselor on a youth retreat that her daughter was attending. The mother corrected her daughter for every little thing during the retreat. The problem was compounded when she did the correcting in front of the youth group. I had to pull the mother aside and ask her to ease up on her daughter. We agreed to focus her attention on the other youth in the group and let the other counselors attend to her daughter.

A father taught a Sunday School class in the same department with his teenage daughter. They had a great relationship, and there were no problems with this combination. The teacher for his daughter's class treated her the same as other girls in the group. There were no problems with other teachers correcting the daughter in front of the father. In fact, several of the other girls thought it was neat to have their friend's father working with the group.

Occasionally, I have had youth threaten to drop out if their parents are in the same group. A boy once said, "If my parents go on the retreat then I'm not going." He looked surprised when I answered, "That's too bad. We're going to have a great time on the retreat. By the way, what were you planning to do that you didn't want your parents to know about?"

We laughed about the situation and talked about the role his parents would play on the retreat. I put his parents with a different group on the retreat and assured him that his parents would not be looking over his shoulder every moment. I talked with the parents, and we all enjoyed the retreat.

When a youth threatens to drop out if his parents are involved, it may signal a deeper problem in the home. At other times, this may only be a way of "saving face" in front of friends. The teenager may fear that the parents are trying to control every move and not allow him any freedom.

A discussion with the parents about ground rules for the youth activity can avoid many of the problems between parents and their own teenagers. Help the parents to approach their responsibilities as *youth leaders* instead of *parents*. For the period they are serving as youth leaders they must be able to relate to their own son or daughter as another youth. They must be willing to allow their teenager the same freedoms as other youth in the group. Save the parent-youth role for the home.

Parents can be involved in youth ministry on many levels if they are selected and enlisted wisely. They have an awareness of the developmental stage of adolescence that can be enriched through appropriate training. Parents, like other adults who work with youth, should be enlisted, trained, equipped, and encouraged to use their spiritual gifts in ministry with youth. It can be a rewarding experience for both parents and youth.

8

Developing the Leadership Team

Any youth minister who attempts to lead single-handedly will discover the frustration of overwhelming needs in ministry. One person can relate to only a limited number of teenagers. Some youth may not like the way you comb your hair, say hello, or blink your eyes. No matter how hard you try, you may never be able to reach that young person. But another adult might be able to reach that youth, develop a relationship, and guide that youth toward Christian maturity. A wise youth minister will learn the fine art of enlisting and equipping youth leaders in order to multiply the ministry, accomplish more, and reach more youth. It is the biblical way.

Youth ministry is a team effort. On the broadest scale the whole church is a youth leadership team. In everyday practice, however, a team of youth leaders carry out the work of youth ministry. The youth minister is in the position to help or hinder development of team unity among youth leaders. The following suggestions can help youth leaders develop team spirit.

Meet Regularly for Planning and Goal Setting

Before they see themselves as real team members, youth leaders must feel they have valuable input into the total youth ministry. Meeting to dream dreams and make plans aids team building. Sunday School workers need to meet weekly to plan for Bible study, outreach, and ministry. Other youth leaders also need regular meetings to plan the work of their groups. All youth leaders need to meet at least quarterly for calendar planning and discussion about upcoming youth events. In a larger church the youth minister should also meet with key leaders on a regular basis for information and input.

Use Leaders in Decision Making and Problem Solving

Team spirit grows when youth leaders feel an ownership of the youth ministry. This involves solving problems and making decisions about their areas of youth ministry. A youth minister needs to make many administrative decisions, but youth leaders should be consulted

59

whenever possible about decisions or problems related to their area of work.

Select Leaders with Differing Viewpoints

We all have a tendency to choose friends who think and react like us. But fresh viewpoints from people who see things differently foster team spirit. It may take some time to help people accept others who think differently, but the benefit is worth the effort. Encourage people to value the opinions of those who differ from them and your youth ministry will gain vitality and sparkle.

Spend Time with Leaders

The best way to develop friendships is to spend time with people. Youth leaders enjoy the friendship of others with common interests and goals. Spend time over coffee, in telephone calls, through written notes, and in personal visits with youth leaders. Take a few moments to shake hands, exchange a few words of cordial conversation, and nurture the friendship of youth leaders.

Build a Spirit of Community

Youth leaders have needs. They are often expected to give with few opportunities to receive. Youth may forget to thank their adult leaders. Be sensitive to ministry needs among youth leaders and help other youth leaders address those needs. Pray for each other during regular planning meetings. Write letters of affirmation and encouragement. Visit the leaders or their family members when they are sick and hospitalized. Notice accomplishments, birthdays, and significant events in the lives of youth leaders.

Share the Spotlight

Youth leaders often go unnoticed. A youth leader who labors faithfully for years deserves a feature article in the church newsletter or a youth handout. Posters or bulletin boards can spotlight individuals or groups of youth leaders. Let youth leaders preside when youth take part in special worship times or youth recognitions in church services. Let those who work with twelfth graders, for example, lead the congregation in recognizing high school seniors at graduation. Let youth leaders teach Bible study sessions during camps or retreats, lead recreational activities, and lead youth fellowships. The youth minister who shares the spotlight with youth leaders will build a stronger youth ministry team.

Provide Money for Youth Leaders

Most churches that have a youth ministry will have some sort of budget for that ministry. The budget can develop a good team spirit. If the youth minister guards the budget and allows it to be used only for those activities he or she plans, then volunteer youth leaders feel powerless to do special projects. A better approach is to provide a portion of the budget funds for the use of their groups. If you want the Sunday School departments to sponsor fellowships for their groups then set aside some funds for them to use. The amount does not have to be large—acknowledging their work will develop better team spirit.

Help Youth Leaders See Results of Their Ministry

Youth ministry does not provide many opportunities for immediate reward. Youth do not line up after Bible study to thank the teacher for the fine job of teaching, the time spent preparing the lesson, or faithful attendance. Adults who volunteer to serve in youth ministry need to be prepared for few immediate rewards, but the rewards are there. A few years later, when the young adult returns to thank the teacher of junior high girls for the work she did and the patience she had with her class, then the rewards make it all worthwhile. Teachers sometimes need the assurance that their work is not in vain. Many youth teachers feel frustrated and defeated. They think that everyone else is doing a better job. They wonder if any youth is gaining anything from their work. A few words of encouragement and assurance will sustain a teacher through moments of questioning and doubts.

Celebrating Together

Some of the warmest times in my ministry have been spent with brothers and sisters who have given of themselves in youth ministry. All the planning, dreaming, working, overcoming difficulties, and serving God together call for moments of celebration, remembering God's dealings with His people, recalling the fun and joy, victories and setbacks, and challenges and the results of faithful obedience to God. It is a moment of worship.

These times can be as simple as a few minutes of handshakes and smiles, or as elaborate as a special meal and recognition time. Recently, I attended a Christmas party for youth workers at our church. During the fun of the evening I reflected on the *koinonia* among the youth leaders and our youth minister. This time of warmth and congeniality brought our youth leadership team together and developed a closer team spirit. Youth leaders can be brought together by celebrating at special times and throughout the year.

9

The Youth Leader's Covenant

The Purpose of a Covenant

Enlisting youth leaders can seem like recruiting people for military service. The recruiting officer might explain the benefits of foreign travel, exciting destinations, and a snappy uniform. But he might forget to mention that boot camp and some undesirable duties can also be part of the deal.

There is a danger in selling the glamor and fun of youth ministry without telling the whole story. People deserve to know what commitments they are making. They deserve to know what is expected of them. They deserve to know what kind of support and training is available.

A youth leader's covenant that spells out the amount of time, type of duties, and level of performance lets the leader know up front what is expected. It paints a more realistic picture of the challenges and fulfillment that are part of youth leadership. It serves as a motivation for leaders to improve their involvement in all areas of service.

Misunderstandings and poor performance on the part of volunteers can often be avoided by using a covenant during the enlistment process. In some ways, the covenant serves as a contract between the leader and the church. It describes how each party—the volunteer leader, the congregation, and the church staff member—will serve together in mutual support. For example, a youth leader may not come to planning meetings regularly. It is difficult to say, *after* they have been enlisted to teach, that youth teachers are expected to attend planning meetings. It is easier to point this out in a covenant during the enlistment process. Then the volunteer leader can be gently reminded of his commitment if he fails to attend planning meetings on a regular basis.

Steps to Developing a Covenant

A church may already have several expectations for those who serve in leadership positions. For example, they must be Christians and members of the church, regular in attendance, and of good moral character. These general statements can easily be incorporated into a leader's covenant. The first step in developing a covenant is to study church policies concerning volunteer leaders.

The next step is to meet with those who are already serving as volunteer youth leaders. A good starting point is to brainstorm elements to be included in the covenant. Ask questions like:

- What are some characteristics of a good youth leader?
- What kinds of things should youth teachers do?
- How much training should be required?
- What kind of support should the church provide?
- How much should the leader be involved in the total church?
- What should the youth minister be expected to do to help the volunteer leaders?

These questions serve as a launching pad for shaping the covenant. Leaders reflect on the responsibilities and challenges of service in youth ministry. In addition, they feel a more vital part of the endeavor and become motivated to better service.

The third step is to make a rough draft of the covenant. State the duties, responsibilities, and expectations of youth leaders using the information gained from church policies and brainstorming sessions. State these elements in a positive manner as much as possible. Include statements about the nature of youth ministry and ways the church and youth minister will support volunteer leaders.

Next, meet with volunteer leaders to review the rough draft of the document. Polish the wording and make changes as needed. Evaluate the items in the document for their impact on present and future volunteers. The covenant should establish a high level of commitment for youth leaders but should not scare off those who are willing to grow into effective workers. Decide if the covenant is to be signed by the volunteers or simply presented to each leader.

Finally, distribute the covenant to each person who is presently serving. Ask the leaders to sign the covenant if you designed it that way. Keep copies of the covenant for use in enlisting leaders in the future.

Things to Avoid

The leader's covenant can present problems if it is handled incorrectly. These difficulties can be avoided by taking some simple precautions.

First, involve current leaders as much as possible in developing the covenant. Some leaders may perceive the covenant as a subtle way to remove them from leadership. They may see the covenant as a threat instead of a statement of support.

Second, help leaders see the covenant as an agreement instead of a measuring stick. Some people are quick to notice their own limitations and do not feel they can live up to a written standard of performance. They may simply resign rather than work to improve, because they do not feel adequate as a youth leader. Be sensitive to low self-esteem among youth leaders. Make sure the statements in the covenant are written in a positive manner.

Third, avoid using the covenant as a hammer to hold over the heads of leaders. True, a leader's covenant is useful in supervising volunteer workers, but it can become a source of anxiety if it is used too often in reminding leaders of their obligations. Youth leaders should be encouraged to serve in response to God's prompting in their lives, not because they signed a document when they were enlisted.

These problems do not have to occur. A leader's covenant should not be imposed on volunteer workers. Rather, it should be a statement of commitments made by those who desire to serve God through youth ministry. If handled with Christian love, developed with a high level of input from present leaders, and used appropriately in the enlistment process, a leader's covenant can be a useful tool for building a team of caring committed adult youth leaders.

A Sample Leader's Covenant

The following is a sample covenant designed for teachers in the Bible teaching program. Other covenants could be developed for directors of departments, outreach leaders, secretaries, discipleship leaders, and so forth.

Responsibilities of Teachers in Youth Sunday School

1. Be a church member.
2. Be regular and punctual in attendance, and in case of unavoidable absence, give notice to director as far in advance as possible.
3. Attend weekly workers meetings.
4. Thoroughly prepare for Sunday's lesson and other duties during the week.
5. Love and enjoy being with young people.
6. Visit in the home of each class member during the first two months of the new year.
7. Individually share the plan of salvation with each class member as needed and encourage spiritual growth in members.
8. Be involved in weekly outreach and visitation to prospects and class members and involve youth in visitation.
9. Coordinate class activities.
10. Be responsible for creating a positive learning environment.

11. Attend special training seminars for youth workers (local, associational, state, and national events).

12. Be loyal to the program of the church, striving to attend all worship services.

10

Creating a Climate of Motivation

The quarterly planning meeting for our youth leaders was under way. We had just finished our meal and opened our calendars to plan for the coming months. I noticed several workers ready to join in the conversation and eagerly anticipating the plans we had made. Others sat on the fringes, only partially attentive, glancing at their watches, waiting for the meeting to end. Many of these had begun to miss planning meetings and arrive late for the classes they taught in church. What was the difference? Why were some obviously motivated and others just enduring the work? What could I do to build interest and motivation?

Anyone who has been in a position of leadership has had to contend with these questions. There are no simple answers. However, understanding motivation can provide insight and some possible answers for those who lead youth ministry.

Keys to Effective Motivation

Reginald McDonough offers practical ways to build a climate for motivation.[3] He identifies four keys to effective motivation.

Stability

People are more highly motivated in a climate in which they feel physically and emotionally secure. This refers to the need for physical safety and emotional safety. The threat of change produces a fear in many people that is as strong as a threat to their physical well-being. People who feel emotionally insecure and threatened by the possibility of unwelcome change will react by fighting, withdrawing in fear, or becoming apathetic. None of these reactions contribute to a healthy climate for motivation. McDonough states: "Persons are more highly motivated in a climate in which there is order, predictability, structure, and stability."

Two examples illustrate how stability creates motivation. In the first case, the youth minister had been reminding the youth teachers of the importance of preparing for their lessons for Sunday School. He had made it clear that the leaders should study and prepare well so the time on Sunday morning would be used in the best way. On Sunday morning, however, the youth minister takes half the period to promote upcoming youth activities. The following week the teachers are told that all youth will meet in the auditorium for a rally during Sunday School. But on Sunday morning the youth minister decides to delay the rally until the next week and sends the youth to their regular classes. The teachers are frustrated because they do not know what to expect or how to prepare for their classes.

In another example, the youth are told they must complete several training classes to take part in the summer mission project. The pastor's son does not participate in any of the training but decides during the last week before the trip that he wants to go with the group. The adult leader tells him he cannot go, and he goes to the youth minister. In this case the youth minister stands by the previous agreement and does not allow the boy to participate. She explains the situation to the pastor, and he supports her decision. The morale of the adult leaders and the youth who have been trained for the mission project is strengthened because the prior agreements have been kept. The rules were not changed arbitrarily, and there is a better sense of stability.

Teamwork

People are more highly motivated when they feel they are in the right position and belong to an exciting, dynamic team. The leaders who are actively involved and sense a spirit of teamwork with other youth leaders will be the most keenly motivated. Those who feel like they are a vital part of the team will form the core of the youth leadership. Those who are on the fringes of the action are most likely to drop out. McDonough states: *Persons are more highly motivated in a climate where they feel a vital part of a team with a significant mission.*

The youth ministry scheduled a retreat and enlisted several youth leaders as sponsors. During the retreat, however, the youth minister taught all the Bible studies, led all the games, and led all the music. The youth leaders sat by and helped clean up after the group sessions. They felt unneeded and out of place. The youth minister missed an opportunity to make them feel like a vital part of the retreat.

Affirmation

People are more highly motivated when they feel appreciated and encouraged. People need to be told they are doing a good job. Honest input about areas that need improvement is also important. Empty flattery can be worse than no communication at all. Look for good things and give honest, sincere praise for the service performed by volunteers. McDonough states: *Persons are more highly motivated in a climate where their sense of self-worth is affirmed and enhanced.*

The youth minister often went to youth leaders on Sunday and offered a word of encouragement and appreciation for their work. He wrote letters, made phone calls, and spoke individually with the leaders. Every leader sensed that he or she was important and had something valuable to contribute to the youth ministry. The youth leaders often met together for fellowship, planning, and sharing joys and frustrations. The youth minister was building a climate for effective motivation by encouraging and affirming the volunteer leaders.

Challenge

Persons are more highly motivated when they sense a high calling from God and find an outlet for expressing their love for God through service and self giving. This key to motivation refers to a person's need for purpose, meaning, and achievement in worthwhile ways. People will respond to a challenge when they recognize their God-given gifts, sense a vision in which those gifts can be used, and are enabled to move toward accomplishing that vision. McDonough states: *Persons are more highly motivated in a climate where they are challenged to develop their full potential and to commit their energies to meaningful ideals and objectives.*

The youth leaders gathered for the regular quarterly planning meeting. Excitement and enthusiasm saturated the group because they each shared a little about their work the previous three months. They also listed plans for their groups in the next few months. Then the youth minister shared plans for the total youth ministry for the next few months. Discussions followed and people were invited to give input. Finally, the youth minister challenged the group to give their best to work toward the goals they had discussed. He followed up by contacting individuals and inviting them to take the leadership roles for several of the major projects. This group of youth leaders is highly motivated because they have a vision of an exciting youth ministry and feel their gifts and energies can be used in meaningful ways.

These four keys provide effective ways for developing a climate of motivation. They work in the church as well as the worlds of business, education, and politics. But the Christian has an extra resource for motivation. That resource is prayer.

God freely invites us to look to Him for resources. "Call to Me, and I will answer you, and I will tell you great and mighty things, which you do not know" (Jer. 33:3). Prayer is the youth minister's most important resource in building a climate for motivation. The working of the Holy

Spirit in the lives of volunteer youth leaders is the extra dimension that surpasses all our human efforts at motivation. Prayer should saturate all we do in youth ministry. It is so much more than simply pleading for God to bless our efforts. It is the starting point, the compass for our directions, and the link to the power for all that we do in God's service.

11

Supervising Volunteer Leaders

Few responsibilities of ministry are as feared or neglected as supervision. Reginald McDonough says, "Traditionally, there has been little or no supervision of the volunteer staff in church organizations. This situation exists for at least three reasons: faulty concepts of supervision, a lack of self-confidence and self-esteem, and a lack of supervisory skills."[4]

Supervision is often avoided in the work of the church. It may be all right for the business world or industry, but not for the church. But this faulty thinking is built around the concept of supervision as a boss controlling every action and laying down the rules. In reality, this style of supervision is out of date and not effective in industry or the church.

Younger youth ministers often hesitate to supervise volunteer youth leaders who are older or more experienced. They avoid supervision because of a lack of self-confidence. Some do not supervise effectively because they lack the self-esteem to face conflicts. It takes a strong ego to rebound after an angry church member attacks you or your work. In either case, people who work together can function more effectively if someone enables the group to move together toward common goals.

Finally, people hesitate to supervise because they do not know how. Supervision calls for an array of skills in leading, listening, negotiating, communicating, and understanding human nature. Many of these skills have to be honed through experience, and trial and error is a hard way to learn.

When people work together, cooperation and understanding is necessary. Proper supervision can help avoid many problems that crop up in youth ministry. Logistical problems occur when different groups use the same room at different times. When a Sunday School department schedules a picnic the same day the youth choir schedules a special rehearsal you can expect frustration and hard feelings among both leaders and youth. Other problems between leaders, areas of responsibilities, choice of curriculum materials, and relationships with youth can be avoided with good supervision. Supervision is not exerting power; it is a ministry of servanthood and support.

Techniques of Supervision

McDonough says that ministers should know certain fundamental techniques in supervision. The following techniques assist in developing effective supervision skills.[5]

Work Through People, Not Around Them

Some of the fondest memories I have are of the relationships with volunteer leaders with whom I have served in youth ministry. Informal fellowships with youth leaders build relationships that improve work conditions and increase emotional ties. Youth leaders sense that they are an important part of the team and eagerly participate in the work.

On the other hand, working around a volunteer leader creates problems. The youth leader may be embarrassed if the workers in his unit receive information before he does. He constantly has to play catchup. If he is routinely passed by without good reason, he may wonder if he is the real leader. Volunteers will begin to feel unneeded. They will feel little or no responsibility for the success of the work. It may seem more efficient to go around a leader to handle a situation, but this can lead to disaster in the long run.

Give Authority Equal to Responsibility

Delegation involves risk. If you enlist someone to do a job, he should be able to complete the task. This means you must trust him to do the task without peering over his shoulder at every move. If you cannot trust him to do the job, then enlist someone else. At the same time, certain restrictions may exist, and these should be communicated when the task is delegated.

Clarify Your Expectations

When a leader is enlisted, there should be a clear explanation of the duties and responsibilities involved. This is where a leader's covenant can be helpful. Each volunteer leader should be enlisted by the person who will supervise him. When a person is enlisted, he should understand clearly what he will be expected to do. A youth minister or church nominating committee should still cultivate prospective leaders. But the leader most directly related to the volunteer should make the actual enlistment. For example, the youth minister should enlist division or department directors in Sunday School. These directors should enlist teachers and other workers in their departments.

Confront Problems, Not People

Problems occur in any organization. The most difficult problem for a youth minister and adult leaders is performance. A good rule of thumb is to focus on the problem rather than the person. If a youth leader has not carried through with a responsibility, then ask, "What can I do to help with this situation?" This is better than saying, "Why haven't you done your job?" People tend to become defensive, and the discussion can quickly turn personal and painful. Keep attention on the problem rather than the person. Create a feeling that the two of you are working together on a common goal and open the door for the leader to grow in responsibility in the future.

Handle Problems Promptly

Do not run from problems, instead run toward them. Ignoring problems will not make them go away. Some problems do seem to work themselves out, but most problems fester and grow into bigger problems. Many problems are the result of gossip, misunderstandings, and petty feelings that were not handled promptly. Most problems can be defused before they become explosive if they are handled in the early stages.

Give Recognition for a Job Well Done

People form their sense of self-esteem when they feel that they have done a job well. Affirmation and encouragement are important, especially in a position with no salary. Public recognition is good, but private praise is even better. A written note, phone call, or personal word to a volunteer leader can build the worker's self-esteem and show your appreciation for a job well done.

Stand Up for Your Leaders

Passing the buck is not good, regardless of the direction it goes. It is wrong to publicly criticize or blame those who supervise you. It is equally wrong to blame those who serve with you. Stand up for those who work under you, and they will stand up for you. Be especially careful to stand by decisions or agreements made with a leader when someone from the power structure becomes critical of the leader.

Check on It and Leave It There

Give a leader the freedom to complete an assignment after it is delegated. There is a temptation to jump in, pick up an unfinished task, and complete the job. This communicates your lack of trust and increases dependence on you to finish all the jobs you have delegated.

Check on assignments, but hold the workers accountable for finishing the job.

Let Leaders Participate in Decision Making

Allow workers to take part in making decisions, and they will sense ownership for accomplishing the task. If decisions are made for them, the leaders may feel no need to carry out the jobs. Participating in decision making increases motivation.

Use Participative Leadership to Create Teamwork

Participative leadership involves leaders by seeking their input, sharing your ideas with them, and enlisting them in problem solving. This kind of leadership creates a sense of teamwork and also develops creativity and freshness.

Lead Workers to Set Goals and Evaluate Programs

This can be one of the thorniest issues of supervision because it leads to personal evaluation. Youth leaders should be involved in setting goals and evaluating progress toward those goals for the entire youth ministry. This creates teamwork and motivation to be involved in the overall ministry. But it also implies that individuals have goals as part of the youth leadership team. This calls for some form of evaluation of personal performance.

Approach the matter of personal evaluation from a supportive, informal stance. Meet privately with each leader to discuss the overall youth ministry and his or her part in the work. Use the following questions to guide your discussion and help the leader become better equipped to serve in youth ministry:

- How do you feel we have been doing this year?
- How do you feel things are going for you in your area?
- What are some areas that you feel good about?
- Are there some areas that need improvement?
- How could I help you do your work better?
- Do you have some personal goals for the coming year?
- Do you have suggestions for my work in our youth ministry?

What About the Ineffective Leader?

What can be done when you have tried everything and a leader is still ineffective? Any leader with volunteers will face this situation at some time. Here are several ideas for handling this problem:

Confront the Issue Directly

Go to the leader and discuss the matter person to person. Explain your concerns and talk about alternatives. Often the volunteer will be relieved to have the problem out in the open for a frank discussion. The leader may be looking for the opportunity to resign and not know how to approach you about the matter. If a person is not doing a good job, he may be unhappy and willing to move to another position.

Salvage the Situation If Possible

Team the ineffective worker with more capable leaders. The positive model of other volunteer youth leaders may help a worker see good youth ministry in action.

Discuss the Matter with Appropriate Persons

If a leader does not want to resign or make improvements, do not try to deal with the matter alone. Discuss the situation with appropriate staff members or church committees. This will avoid giving the impression that you have a personal grudge against someone and will provide support if the leader appeals the decision.

Deal with the Matter

Do not allow one ineffective leader to stagnate the entire youth ministry. Though confronting the problem can be painful, one negative youth leader can harm many others and hurt the total youth ministry. If the leader does not offer to resign and shows no willingness to improve, then for the good of the overall youth ministry, ask for his resignation directly.

12

Interns and Assistants

Using interns and assistants is a growing trend, especially among larger youth ministries. College and seminary students provide an additional source of leadership and learn youth ministry on a first-hand basis. Some interns serve for a summer while others serve for a semester, a school year, or twelve months. Interns may be paid staff or volunteers. Assistants are normally paid at least a part-time salary.

Why Use Interns?

The New Testament suggests the reason for using interns. First, Christ chose twelve who were called to be with Him, learn from Him, and continue the work He started. They did little to build the kingdom of God while Christ was living among them. In fact, they often stumbled in their efforts and held back the work Jesus was doing. But their ministry blossomed after Christ ascended to heaven and sent the Holy Spirit to work through them. The teachings of Christ and first-hand experience as part of His earthly ministry thrust them into key leadership roles under the power of the Holy Spirit.

Second, Paul commanded young Timothy, "The things which you have heard from me in the presence of many witnesses, these entrust to faithful men, who will be able to teach others also" (2 Tim. 2:2). Youth ministers have a responsibility not only to lead youth ministry today, but to equip others to assume leadership in the future.

Developing the Intern Program

The first task in developing an intern program is to determine the purpose and length of an internship. Is it going to be a summer program for a college student? Or, is it a semester or year-long program? Will it be an experiment, or is this a permanent position? Is this going to be a paid or volunteer position? Will the student intern be working for academic credit at a college or seminary?

Discuss the purpose of internships by considering the relationship of the intern to the youth minister, other church staff, and volunteer leaders. Will the intern attend church staff meetings? Will the intern supervise any volunteer leaders? Will the intern work on jobs as assigned or will he or she have a specific area of responsibility? Who supervises the intern?

Determine the number of interns needed and the amount to pay each one. A simple rule of thumb is to add one intern when the youth enrollment reaches 250 or more. Then add one intern for each additional 125 youth. Paying the interns will depend on the financial resources of the church.

A job description and list of specific responsibilities should be determined before enlisting interns or assistants. The pastor, church personnel committee, and others involved in staff supervision should be fully aware of the intern position. Secure appropriate approval before interviewing anyone for the job.

Some churches have great potential for interns because they are situated near college or seminary campuses. Others must travel a long distance to find available interns. Think through the program before announcing the position. Then prepare for interviewing candidates and selecting the right person for the job.

Interviewing Interns

Prepare written materials that describe the job, salary, length of service, and specific expectations. Make this material and information about your church available to the candidates. An application form is useful for screening, especially if you interview several people.

Watch for pitfalls during the interviewing process. The first danger is picking the wrong person. Many college or seminary students have great zeal for the Lord but lack any desire to work with youth. They may be looking for a job without sensing a call to youth ministry. Youth ministry should be more than a stepping-stone or source of employment. It demands the best from a person called and gifted by God to youth ministry. Ask specific questions about the person's motivation to serve in the youth ministry position.

Second, people usually try to make the best impression and mask shortcomings during an interview. Check references to determine the person's Christian life-style, skills in relating to people, and past work records.

In addition, consider how the candidate will fit into your church situation. Are there specific skills or gifts that are needed? Is there a need for a male or female in the position? How will you feel about working alongside this person? Will the volunteer leaders accept this person?

Finally, does the person indicate a willingness to stick with the job and learn from the experience? If the term of the internship is a semester or a year, the candidate should be willing to remain in the position throughout the length of the internship.

The application form should ask for the following information:

GENERAL: Name, address, telephone, date of birth.

FAMILY: Parents' name and address, marital status of candidate, some information about family background, and relationship to the church.

CHURCH: Present church affiliation, pastor's name and address, other church membership in the past, church activities, volunteer and paid staff experience.

EDUCATION: Schools attended and diplomas or degrees earned, school activities, areas of study, special skills, vocational intent.

HEALTH: General questions about height, weight, physical condition, disabilities, and medications.

EMPLOYMENT: Employment record including dates, length of employment, and reason for leaving.

PERSONAL: General questions concerning strengths and weaknesses, Christian life-style, statement of conversion, and statement of a call to ministry.

DOCTRINAL: Some questions concerning specific doctrinal issues may be desired by your church.

REFERENCES: Pastor, personal friends, instructors or professors, and employers.

Training and Accountability

A contract may be desirable when an intern is chosen. This form should describe the length of service, salary, hours of work each week, and other responsibilities as you desire. If a contract is not used, then a record of employment such as the minutes of a personnel committee's actions or a congregational vote should be used to indicate the formal action of the church.

Specific goals help the intern by providing direction and focus to his or her work. The first days on the job should be spent orienting and training the person. Personal appearance and conduct, office routines, introduction to other church staff members, weekly schedules, and specific areas of responsibilities should be discussed at this time. Spend time laying the foundation, and the intern will be better equipped to be an effective leader.

Weekly report forms are often used to guide the work of interns. These provide both direction and accountability. The report forms also help in evaluating progress during the internship.

Reports are usually submitted to the youth minister, other church staff, church personnel committee, and pastor. Even though all staff members may not read every report, this procedure builds a sense of accountability for the intern.

Here are some items that can be found on weekly intern report forms:

- Campus visits—The specific schools visited by the intern and contacts with youth at the school.
- Prospect visits—Names and results of visits made to youth who are prospective members.
- New Christian visits—Names and results of visits made to youth who are new Christians. This provides follow-up for new Christians and guides them to baptism.
- Relationship visits—Names and results of visits made to youth for the purpose of building personal relationships.
- Plans and goals—Weekly plans, goals, events, and activities. This is a good place for personal evaluation of progress by the intern.

Interns can be worthwhile additions to a youth ministry. They provide youthful energy and creativity. They can make possible innovative approaches that go beyond the normal resources of the church. Internships give priceless learning experiences for future youth ministers.

Part 3
Youth Ministry with Youth

13

Adolescents as Persons

Approximately 19.5 million youth (grades seven to twelve) live in the United States. Over the next five years, this number will grow to about 21.5 million.[1] Seventy-four percent of thirteen to fifteen-year-old youth say that religion is either the most important or one of the most important influences in their lives. Ninety-five percent of thirteen to fifteen-year-old youth say they believe in "God or a universal spirit."[2]

A desire to reach, teach, disciple, and minister to these young persons offers a channel of service that promises fulfillment and joy. This section deals with the heart of youth ministry. The call to serve God through ministry with youth first expresses itself through a love for teenagers.

We see youth laughing, crying, singing, playing, talking, helping, hurting, and exhibiting the youthful energy of dreams on the threshold of adulthood. Teenagers in all their moods and potential cry out to us for ministry. The haunting song of the challenge of adolescence is the entry ramp to a life of ministry with youth.

Describing Youth

How shall we describe these wonderful creatures we call teenagers? They stand in the in-between world, neither child nor adult. Yet they are not some half-baked object that is neither this nor that. To say they are "in-between" sounds like they lack something that characterizes "normal" people.

Teenagers are first and foremost human beings. They are more than the descriptions we attach like labels. They are persons created by God. As such, they have needs and potential for ministry.

To minister to teenagers, we must try to understand them. How shall we minister if we do not know to whom we minister? How can we affirm and guide and shape if we do not understand to some degree the persons and context of ministry?

One way to describe teenagers is *developmentally*. Developmental terms like puberty, adolescence, moodiness, identity development, and self-image have been used in efforts to gain an understanding of this age group.

Another way to describe teenagers is *sociologically*. When we talk about cliques, peer pressure, social development, gangs, dating, friendships, parent-teen relationships, and the church youth group, we are attempting to picture teenagers in sociological terms.

Another way to describe teenagers is *culturally*. Even the word *teen-ager* is a cultural term since it means more than simply the years in a person's life. It speaks of the culture in which we live. When we speak of teenage fads, music, slang, subculture, hangouts, generation gap, and rebellion, we say something about our culture.

Still another way to describe teenagers comes to us through images from the media—television, movies, magazines, and music. The picture we see most often of teenagers is an exaggerated exploitation of adolescence. The extremes of rebellion, vandalism, silliness, nerdi-ness, soft-core pornography, hedonistic life-style, and general lack of purpose in life appear to be way the media sees teens. Adolescents become cartoon characters rather than realistic persons. These representations color our perceptions and shape how we minister with teenagers. We must help those who minister with youth and their families to see a clearer, more valid picture of adolescents.

Youth Are Human Beings

When we describe the group we call *teenagers*, we sometimes seem to suggest that teenagers are somehow different from other people. The more we focus the microscope on adolescents, the less we see them in light of the entire life cycle. We need to see youth in the context of other age groups and social relationships.

Youth are human beings. They are born, grow and develop, relate to God and other human beings, live their lives, and suffer the maladies and afflictions of all human beings. With all their distinctives, they still have more in common with other people than we often recognize.

Looking at the Total Life

Two episodes from the life of Jesus emphasize that adolescence should be viewed as part of the entire span of life. The first episode comes at the close of the trip to Jerusalem (Luke 2:41-52). The twelve-year-old Jesus had remained behind in Jerusalem when the family began the journey back to Nazareth. Joseph and Mary had to search for their Son for three days. After locating Jesus in the temple, sitting with the teachers, Mary asked Him why He had done this. Jesus reminded His mother of this relationship with His Heavenly Father (vv.

48-50). Then the Gospel writer says that Jesus continued in subjection to His earthly parents (v. 51), and He kept developing in "wisdom, and stature, and in favor with God and men" (v. 52). Jesus grew and developed in all facets of life—physically, mentally, emotionally, socially, and spiritually.

A second episode underscores the need to view human development in its totality of growth and relationships. A scribe came to Jesus with a question about the greatest commandment (Mark 12:28). Verses 29-31 tells us Jesus answered with the traditional *Shema*, "Hear, O Israel! The Lord our God is One Lord; and you shall love your God with all your heart, and with all your soul, and with all your mind, and with all your strength" (Deut. 6:4-5). But then He added, "You shall love your neighbor as yourself" (Lev.19:18). Jesus stated clearly that all facets of human development are important—intellectual, emotional, volitional, and physical. The social relationships with other people are important, as is the spiritual relationship with God.

These two examples from the life of Jesus give several clues to understanding teenagers. First, consider all facets of life in teenagers, not just the spiritual aspects. Those who work with youth in church sometimes look only at the ways youth are involved in youth activities and ignore other dimensions of life. We cannot separate Sunday morning from Saturday night. What happens to teenagers Monday through Saturday has as much bearing on their lives as what happens to them Sunday evening at an after-church fellowship.

A second clue to a better understanding of teenagers is to consider youth in light of their many social relationships. Parents, friends, other relatives, teachers, and bosses shape the ways teenagers grow up. We may know the average age of puberty in adolescents, types of physical changes that happen to teenagers, and ways they mature intellectually. But if we ignore the impact of the network of family, friends, and other adults on youth, we paint a limited picture of adolescence.

Finally, we must consider the need teenagers have for loving relationship with God, family, other church members, and the world around them. We often picture teenagers as living in their own subculture, isolated from generations before and after them. Peers are extremely important to youth, but they do not represent all of life. Teens long for acceptance and approval from their parents and other significant adults. A church will never have a strong youth ministry unless there are adults who love and nurture youth, even though those adults have little connection with youth program organizations or activities.

God's love and care for all people is most clearly seen in the lives of the members of His family, the church. Nurtured by this network of love and acceptance, youth are enabled to accept God's love and forgiveness and share this message of hope with the lost world.

14

Developmental Tasks of Adolescents

Havighurst's Developmental Tasks

One way to describe adolescents is through a series of tasks that must be accomplished in order to reach the next level of maturity. Robert J. Havighurst is perhaps the best-known proponent of development tasks.[3]

At every stage of maturity, from childhood through adulthood, there are a series of tasks. These are sequential in the sense that one task must be successfully completed before subsequent tasks can be accomplished. Havighurst also believes that there is a critical period during which the tasks can be mastered most easily. Failure to complete the tasks during that period can lead to difficulties in mastering the task later.

Havighurst lists several developmental tasks for adolescents:

1. Accepting one's physique.
2. Accepting an appropriate masculine or feminine role.
3. Achieving emotional and economic independence from parents and other adults.
4. Selecting and preparing for a vocation.
5. Developing intellectual skills and concepts necessary for civic competence.
6. Desiring and achieving socially responsible behavior and preparing for marriage and family life.
7. Achieving new relations with age mates of both sexes.
8. Acquiring a set of values that are in harmony with the social environment.

Erikson's Developmental Phases

Erik Erikson describes the growth process from infancy through the latter years of adulthood.[4] He identifies eight phases of development in terms of a conflict that must be resolved during each particular phase. Every phase involves a crisis that can be resolved by achievement of a sense of some particular competence. Failure to achieve the competence would result in a sense of incompetence in that phase. The first five phases cover the period of infancy and childhood. The last three phases cover the adult years.

Erikson's eight phases of life and corresponding age groups are:

1. Trust versus mistrust (babies)
2. Autonomy versus shame and doubt (young infants)
3. Initiative versus guilt (younger children)
4. Industry versus inferiority (older children)
5. Identity versus role confusion (adolescents)
6. Intimacy versus isolation (young adults)
7. Generativity versus stagnation (middle adults)
8. Ego Integrity versus disgust and despair (older adults)

The fifth phase deals with the period of adolescence. The central task during adolescence is the development of a sense of identity. Although Erikson never defines identity in a simple and straightforward way, he devoted much of his writing to the subject of identity and identity formation. Erikson describes this process when he states:

> In psychological terms, identity formation employs a process of simultaneous reflection and observation, a process taking place on all levels of mental functioning, by which the individual judges himself in the light of what he perceives to be the way in which others judge him in comparison to themselves and to a typology significant to them; while he judges their way of judging him in the light of how he perceives himself in comparison to them and to types that have become relevant to him.[5]

Identity development for adolescents is not so much a *discovery* of identity as it is a *commitment* to the potential of who one can become. Teenagers are faced with a multitude of choices in all areas of life. They work through these choices, at least to some extent, through experimentation with different roles of life. Failure to sort through the panorama of selves leads to a confusion of identity that drains energy needed to make significant decisions of adulthood.

Adolescence allows the person making the transition from childhood to adulthood to decide on and pledge fidelity to choices of vocation, life-style, marriage partner, and ultimate allegiance in life. It is a time to commit to "*who* I am" as well as "*whose* I am."

Affirming the Goals of Adolescence

Adolescence can also be seen as a series of goals to be accomplished as one moves toward responsible adulthood. Merton and

Irene Strommen offer a helpful list of seven goals an adolescent intuitively seeks to achieve:[6]

1. Achievement—The satisfaction of arriving at excellence in some area of endeavor.
2. Friends—The broadening of one's social base by having learned to make friends and maintain them.
3. Feelings—The self-understanding gained through having learned to share one's feelings with another person.
4. Identity—The sense of knowing "who I am," of being recognized as a significant person.
5. Responsibility—The confidence of knowing "I can stand alone and make responsible decisions."
6. Maturity—Transformation from a child to an adult.
7. Sexuality—Acceptance of responsibility for one's new role as a sexual being.

The first letters of each of these goals form the acronym *affirms*. This suggests an approach to help youth move toward becoming a responsible adult as we remember these seven goals:

Adolescent Goals

A Achievement realized
F Friends gained
F Feelings understood
I Identity established
R Responsibility accepted
M Maturity gained
S Sexuality understood

An affirming approach is the key concept in understanding and guiding youth. This style of ministry enables youth to make it through the stressful times that will come. It remains positive and affirming because Christ offers a life of promise and hope. It approaches youth ministry by seeing youth as diamonds in the rough, not yet finished and polished, but possessing tremendous promise and potential.

15

Physical Development of Adolescents

Puberty and Physical Changes

Late in childhood the biological alarm clock goes off and puberty arrives. Adolescence begins with the onset of puberty—a complex set of biological and chemical changes in a person's body that mark the end of childhood and beginning of the transition from childhood toward adulthood.

Girls reach puberty about two years earlier than boys. Although there is a range of ages when puberty begins, it generally occurs about ages eleven to twelve for girls and about ages thirteen to fourteen for boys. The following chart shows the normal age ranges of puberty for girls and boys.[7]

One of the most noticeable changes during puberty is the growth spurt. A tremendous amount of growth occurs as the bones and muscles respond to the growth hormones secreted by the pituitary and other endocrinal glands.

The second greatest amount of physical growth in a person's life, exceeded only by the amount of growth in a baby during the first few months following birth occurs at puberty. This growth does not happen smoothly and evenly, however. All the parts of the body do not change at the same rate of speed. The bones grow faster than the muscles, and this creates a great deal of awkwardness and clumsiness. Sometimes it seems that a young person walking through a room can break more things with arms and feet than a martial arts expert!

Puberty is actually an inward change that is visible through outward signs called secondary sex characteristics. For girls, these secondary sex characteristics include: broadening of the hips and pelvic area, experiencing the first menstrual period, enlargement of the breasts, and developing the female body shape and form. For boys, secondary sex characteristics include: changing voice, development of facial and

NORMAL AGE RANGES OF PUBERTY

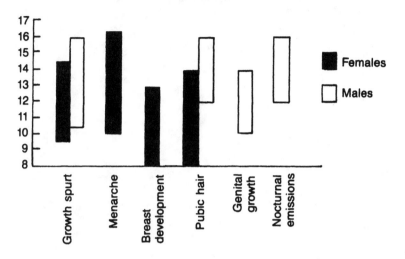

Dacey, 1982 (based on Tanner, 1970; Marshall & Tanner, 1970)

body hair, increasing muscular development, and evidence of the first sperm in the semen.

Early and Late Development

Puberty brings a radical change in a person's physical appearance. This change does not occur at the same time nor at the same rate of speed for all people. Some reach puberty earlier than others, and some grow more rapidly or slowly than their peers. These discrepancies create confusion and anxiety for teenagers as they compare themselves with their classmates at school or some idealized image of what they should look like.

Girls seem to be bothered most when they develop earlier than their peers. Early developing girls have disadvantages in terms of body image, school performance, and school behaviors.[8] They do have advantages in terms of popularity with the opposite sex and allowed independence.

Girls who are "early bloomers" are less likely to earn good grades and/or score well on standardized tests. They are more likely to show behavior problems at school. It is possible that some girls who are the "late bloomers" are less popular with the opposite sex and spend more time with their homework and grades.

Boys who are "early bloomers," on the other hand, have greater satisfaction with their height, muscular development, and athletic abilities than their peers. They also have a more positive attitude about being a boy.[9] Generally, being an early bloomer is an advantage for boys but a disadvantage for girls. Conversely, developing a little later is an advantage for girls but a disadvantage for boys.

16

Social and Emotional Development of Adolescents

Emotional Changes

The teen years are often called the "turbulent teens" because of the moodiness and changeable behaviors of adolescents. Their emotions sometimes resemble roller-coasters. However, a knowledge of the developmental aspects of adolescent emotions will help adults see these emotions in more understandable, predictable ways.

There is a relationship between the level of hormones in the body and the emotions. Women sometimes experience a change in emotions during their monthly menstrual cycle as the hormone level rises and falls. These same feelings occur in adolescents. For early adolescents the hormone level increases about twentyfold after puberty.

Those who work with teenagers should realize that emotions can play tricks on adolescents. Teenagers experience new feelings, and they often do not know how to respond. As a result, emotions can create problems for the young person and anyone within shouting distance.

An emotional outburst by a teenager toward an adult may have little to do with the adult. The teenager may be emotionally stressed because he or she just broke off a relationship, is worried about telling parents of some trouble, was not invited to a party, or is experiencing a new body chemistry. Adults would do well to remember Proverbs 15:1, "A gentle answer turns away wrath, But a harsh word stirs up anger." Giving the emotional youth a little space and time to deal with the problem often results in better feelings for everyone. Above all, adults should not allow a teenager's emotions to dictate their responses.

Adults are sometimes puzzled by a teenager's emotions. Parents often wonder, *Why does she act that way?* A recent study of younger adolescents and their parents revealed that young adolescents worry most about how they're doing in school, their looks, and how their friends treat them. Worry about peer relationships grows stronger as the adolescent grows older. Parents often overestimate how deeply their teenager worries about peer relationships.[10]

The chart below shows the top twenty worries of young adolescents in order of their importance to the adolescents. Significant differences appear between boys and girls on eighteen of the items. Worries that girls report more than boys are indicated in the second column. Worries boys report more than girls are indicated in the third column:[11]

Total Group	Girls	Boys
• My school performance	X	
• My looks	X	
• How well other kids like me	X	
• That one of my parents might die	X	
• How my friends treat me	X	
• Hunger and poverty in the U. S.	X	
• Violence in the U. S.		
• That I might lose my best friend	X	
• Drugs and drinking around me	X	
• That I might not get a good job		X
• Whether my body is growing normally		
• Nuclear bombing of the U. S.		X
• That my parents might divorce		
• That I may die soon		
• Sexual abuse	X	
• That friends will get me in trouble		X
• Drinking by a parent		X
• Getting beat up at school		X
• Physical abuse by a parent		X
• That I might kill myself		X

The largest differences in worries between boys and girls are in three areas: looks, how well other kids like them, and sexual abuse. There is no difference between boys and girls in their worries about violence in the U. S., whether their body is developing normally, that they might die soon, and that their parents might divorce.[12]

Parents do not always predict the worries of their sons and daughters very well. They tend to *under*estimate the degree of concern their child has for the destructive or hazardous forces of life. Hunger, poverty, and violence are more serious concerns for adolescents, particularly younger adolescents, than their parents presume. On the other hand, parents tend to *over*estimate the level of worry of their child regarding the relationships with their friends.[13]

Emotions can be frustrating to both parents and teens. Learning to deal with new feelings and experiences is a tricky process that creates tension and can lead to arguments, hurt feelings, and grudges between youth and adults. Some emotional outbursts are caused by biological changes while others grow out of worries and concerns. Understanding the causes of some of these emotions can build a spirit of empathy and caring concern. A healthy dose of patience will help parents and youth leaders guide adolescents into more mature ways of handling their emotions.

The Changing Social Scene

During Jan's childhood years the family seemed to be close emotionally. Mother and Father enjoyed laughing and talking with their child, and the rough times never seemed to present any major catastrophes. Wrong behaviors were corrected, and Jan seemed pliable and obedient. Her friends were mostly children of adults who were known by the family. Activities and interests centered around the family. Mom and Dad knew most of Jan's plans and activities.

Then puberty comes. Strange things happen to the family relationships. Mother and Father no longer know all of Jan's friends. Schedules and activities come at a frantic pace. Jan wants to make her own decisions and demands to know "Why?" every time her freedom seem threatened. The heat turns up on the parent-teen relationship.

Friends take on extra meaning to Jan. As she grows older, friends of the opposite sex pay more attention. Meanwhile, Mom and Dad scratch their heads and ask themselves what has happened to their innocent little offspring.

The social changes of adolescence are as radical as the other changes of this period of life. Parents and youth leaders need to understand the social transformations that take place in at least three areas:

- Parent-teen relationships
- Relationships with opposite sex
- Relationships with friends

Parent-Teen Relationships

The teenager lives in two worlds. One world consists of the family (parents, siblings, extended family) and represents the childhood of the adolescent. The other world consists of the peers, acquaintances, and other adults outside the circle of the family. This represents a new world in which the teenager is the expert with more knowledge and information than the parents.

A teenager listens to signals from both worlds, trying to walk a tightrope between the two. Like wearing stereo headphones with signals coming from two sources, the young person attempts to adjust the balance between the two and bring integration of the signals into his or her life experiences. This is not always an easy task.

Parents often misinterpret the teenager's attention to peers as rejection of the parents and family values. As adolescents step toward the world outside the circle of the family, parents may assume their child has stepped completely out of the family circle. Peers seem to have total influence and control of their young person's life. Horror stories of drugs, immoral sexual activities, rebellion, and peer pressures do not ease the parent's fears that their little one is lost and gone forever.

In reality, the parent-teen relationship looks more like the following illustration:

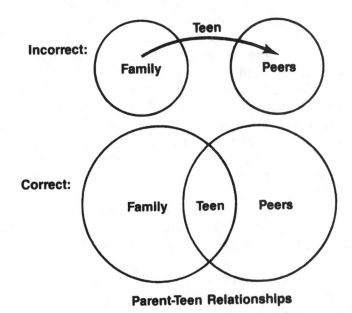

Parent-Teen Relationships

Peers do assume more influence during the adolescent years. But parental influence is still very strong. Continuing research reveals that the strongest influence on the life of a teenager is his or her parents. A Search Institute survey shows that parental influence decreases while peer influence increases each year through the ninth grade but at no time does the peer influence outweigh the influence of parents. This influence was tested over six topics: trouble in school, how to handle feelings, drugs and alcohol, questions about sex, feelings of guilt, and deciding what to with one's life.[14]

Other surveys of teenagers reveal similar results. In a survey by

TeenAge magazine, American young people were asked who or what has the most influence in their lives. Sixty-six percent said family and 27 percent said friends have the most influence.[15] A *USA Today* poll asked young people to whom they would turn if they were caught doing something wrong at school. Parents were the choice for 38 percent of the respondents, followed by friend (32 percent), a counselor (19 percent), a teacher (16 percent), a sibling (6 percent), a boyfriend or girlfriend (4 percent), and a grandparent (2 percent). Another 14 percent responded "other/I don't know."[16]

John J. Conger and Anne C. Petersen note that the values of parents and those of the teenager's peer group are not always at opposite poles. Values usually overlap because of common social, economic, religious, educational, and geographical backgrounds. Conger and Petersen go on to state:

> Peer influence is more likely to be predominant in such matters as tastes in music and entertainment, fashions in clothing and language, patterns of same- and opposite-sex peer interaction, and the like. Parental influence is more likely to be predominant in such areas as underlying moral and social values, and understanding of the adult world. It is also important to recognize that when the peer group assumes an unusually dominant role in the lives of adolescents, often it is due as much, or more, to the lack of attention and concern at home as to the inherent attractiveness of the peer group.[17]

What to Do?

Parents and youth leaders may be puzzled by bizarre behavior that sometimes appears rebellious. Should adults give up and let the tide of adolescence run its course? Or, should they seize control and exert more pressure on the actions and decisions of their teenagers? Here are some suggestions for survival in the changing social world of adolescence:[18]

Learn to Say No

This calls for the fine art of knowing the difference between wants and needs. Youth need reasonable boundaries with freedom to act within those boundaries. Some of the most frustrated teenagers I have known were those from homes where there were no boundaries or where the boundaries constantly changed. Parents and youth leaders sometimes avoid saying no because they want to avoid confrontation. Or, they are told that *everybody* except their teenager gets to do certain things. Learn to deal with principles rather than pressure and act accordingly. A teenager should not do harmful or dangerous things simply because everybody else does them.

Learn to Be Persistent

Recently a parent asked me, "What should I do if I have told my child very clearly to finish her chores before she goes out, and she does not finish her chores but still wants to go out?" The answer is simple. Tell her again! Youth leaders and parents often tell teenagers a couple of times to do something and then give up. We need to be as plodding and persistent as the teenager if he or she is to learn that we cannot be worn down.

Deal with Problems and Move On

Grudges and hurt feelings can bear down on relationships between teens and adults if they are not handled in due time. Harsh words, hurt feelings, broken rules, and inappropriate behavior should be confronted and cleared before they fester into broken relationships.

True, if this happens in a public place or the teenager or adult is not able to handle it emotionally at that minute, a cooling-off period can be helpful. For example, what should parents do if their teenager comes in late and drunk? Perhaps the best thing would be to go to bed and discuss the matter the next day. The worse thing would be to get mad and never deal with the problem. Parents, youth, and youth leaders should learn to clear the air, erase past problems from the blackboard of grudges, and move on.

Keep a Balance Between Standards and Understanding

We do not help teenagers when we brush aside unacceptable behaviors and say, "Ah, they're just being crazy kids." Sometimes hurtful words, bad manners, and harmful actions are just that. There is no deep, mysterious reason behind them.

We help teenagers best by holding reasonable standards and values and expecting them to abide by them. Every action or misdeed is not worthy of all-out war, but some battles are worth fighting. Parents and youth leaders should choose their battles carefully and expect youth to live within certain boundaries. Adults outside the home or youth group will take the youths' actions at face value and will not try too hard to understand their motivations. We can help youth survive in that world by not going to extremes as we try to understand them.

Talk with Them

Communication is a key word, but many times we don't know how to do it. We are told to listen aggressively, and this is important. But we are not told how to talk. As a result, adults do not talk with teenagers very well.

My computer has a modem (a communication device) which I use to "talk" with the high-tech world of computers. I dial a number, make the right settings, punch a few keys, and get the information I need. This works great for computers, but it is a terrible way to approach communication with teenagers.

There is no secret formula for talking and listening between adults and teenagers. We cannot program conversations like computers. We need loving spirits and a lot of time. Sometimes we need to start talking, let the words flow, and allow our teenagers to do the same. Teenagers do not always know what is bothering them. They need to talk freely so they can discover what they are saying. Adults must also listen without interrupting to question or challenge.

Understand the Difference Between Authority and Power

Parental authority is a concept that modern parents often do not understand. Asserting authority differs from exercise power. Power is based on force, while authority is based on wisdom, knowledge, and skill. Parents who pressure their teenagers through badgering, abuse, or threats are not asserting parental authority. They are asserting superior power. A bully has power. A skilled teacher, leader, or surgeon has authority.

David Elkind explains the difference between power and authority:

> Exerting parental authority doesn't mean that we can't play ball with our children or joke with them or have fun with them. Being a parent doesn't mean being an ogre or a relentless disciplinarian. Rather it means asserting ourselves as adults who have more experience, knowledge, and skill than our offspring. Children and teenagers are young and inexperienced. They very much want guidance and instruction from us.[19]

Keep a Sense of Humor

The best parents and youth leaders I know all seem to have one trait in common—a healthy sense of humor. They take their roles seriously, but they do not take themselves too seriously. Many times my wife and I have looked at each other with a smile and reminded ourselves, "This, too shall pass." Remember that the trials and tribulations of parents, teenagers, and youth leaders can be frustrating and troublesome, but they will pass and life will go on. Keep a balance between looking at the troubles of teenagers and the special creativity and charm those teens evoke.

Relationships with the Opposite Sex

Perhaps no greater social change occurs than the discovery of the opposite sex. Dating becomes a fascinating adventure in relationships. Sadly, many teenagers equate dating with a prelude to sexual activity and never really develop the social skills of dating.

Early adolescence is often the time for the first taste of the dating experience. This is a time for such activities as dating, kissing, and falling in love. A Search Institute survey reported that 24 percent of the fifth graders said they had no best friends who were members of the opposite sex. Thirty-one percent of the fifth graders said half or more of their best friends were of the opposite sex. On the other hand, of the ninth graders reporting, only 7 percent said they had no best friends of the opposite sex, while 57 percent said half or more of their best friends were members of the opposite sex.[20]

The percentage of young adolescents who say they are in love increases by grade from the fifth grade upward. The Search Institute study indicates that boys are more likely to report experience with dating and kissing than girls. More fifth graders report being in love, dating, and kissing than adults might expect. Nearly 40 percent report being in love, with more than one in four fifth graders reporting dating and/or kissing in the last twelve months. Between the eighth and ninth grades a major increase takes place in reports of dating and kissing. [21]

A frightening byproduct of this early experience with dating is the number of young adolescents who report having sexual intercourse at least one time. One out of five ninth graders say they have engaged in sexual intercourse at least once. There is a wide difference between boys and girls in this area. Twenty-eight percent of the ninth grade boys say they have had sexual intercourse, while only 13 percent of the girls indicate having sexual intercourse. Among fifth graders, 17 percent (22 percent of the boys and 9 percent of the girls) say they have had sexual intercourse.[22]

These numbers frighten parents and youth leaders. Even more sobering is the point that these figures were gathered from young people with at least some degree of church involvement.

I spent my early childhood in the country, with a dirt road running in front of our house. Neighborhood dogs would chase a car along the road until they almost choked on the cloud of dust. I often wondered what a dog thought was so great about chasing cars. What would he do if he ever caught one?

Dating for younger adolescents is a little like that. The thrill is in the chase, but it can be awkward when two young teenagers are alone and discover they have to *talk* to one another!

Three seventh-grade boys were seated on a rock ledge beside a sidewalk. An attractive twelfth-grade girl had the misfortune of walking along in front of the three boys. They whistled, shouted, made cat-calls, and were generally obnoxious, trying to get the girl's attention. She went her way and ignored the younger boys, while they laughed and kidded each other about their macho good looks.

I laughed to think what they would have done if the girl had turned and approached the three boys. They would have melted in their shoes! It was easy to "chase" her from a safe distance, but she would have intimidated them in a face-to-face encounter.

Adults can help youth keep their dating relationships in perspective by helping youth develop their social skills. Younger youth, especially, feel awkward around peers of the opposite sex. Girls are usually more mature than boys of their same age. Only in the high school years do boys catch up with girls. Even then, they need practice relating to each other on social levels as well as the more romantic levels.

As a rule, avoid getting involved in dating relationships. These can be volatile! I have known youth leaders who try to become match makers, and they always get burned. Youth want to work out their own dating relationships. Adults must be ready to offer guidance and suggestions when asked, but be careful about becoming a dating problem solver.

Relationships with Friends

Friendships hold special meanings to adolescents. Close friends allow the teenager the opportunity to express intimate fears and joys that cannot be shared with others. The peer group provides a context for growth, but friendships contribute to social development in ways the broader peer group cannot. One of the concerns of families looking for a church home is whether or not their teenager will find a friend. Parents often express concern about the type of friends their son or daughter chooses and the amount of time spent with friends.

Friendships during the teen years generally fall into three categories: the crowd, the clique, and best friends. During the childhood years, boys and girls have friends, neighborhood playmates, and acquaintances from school. Many of their school friends also come from the same neighborhood. As the child moves into the adolescent years, the circle of friends grows larger and there are more casual acquaintances. "Where the school aged child's peer group was peopled with friends, best friends and faceless strangers, the adolescent has a wider circle of casual acquaintances as well."[23]

The Crowd

The crowd is the largest and most inclusive of teenage friendships. It is also the most impersonal. This is the group that is thrown together because of the structures of school, church, and other social organizations. Youth find themselves in crowds based on mutual interests, likes, or skills. The football team, band, and school clubs are examples of crowds. The church youth group can be a crowd. The primary function of crowds is to provide a structured organization for *group activities and social interaction between the sexes.*

The Clique

Cliques are smaller groups of more intimate friends, resembling in many ways a family grouping. Cliques may help teenagers make the social transition from the world of family and parents to the world of peers. Although cliques often carry a negative impression, they serve a useful purpose in the social development of teenagers. The primary function of cliques is *talking,* a great deal of that on the telephone. This provides the teenager the opportunity to discuss the activities of the group and exchange ideas about how to respond, dress for the occasion, and understand the social processes of the activity. Cliques serve to provide information about an activity, prepare for the activity, and evaluate the activity after it is over.

A youth group of more than ten people probably will have cliques. While these cliques (smaller groups within the larger group) may become exclusive and cause some to feel left out, they may also help youth feel accepted and comfortable within the larger group. They can be helpful in providing answers about the emerging social world of the teenager. Adults can help youth keep their smaller circles of friends positive and open rather than negative knots that make others feel excluded and uncomfortable.

Best Friends

Teenagers who are trying to adjust to rapidly changing body shapes, new social patterns, and deep emotional urges may often experience doubts, anxieties, and frustrations. To admit them to anyone but the closest friends opens the door for misunderstanding, rejection, or ridicule. Between best friends, however, there is an intimacy and openness that allows honest communication. Trust develops between best friends which allows the two to let down their defenses and sort through the maze of questions and doubts about their development. The primary function of best friends, then is *honest, open communication and understanding at the feeling level.* As one youth expressed it,

"My best friend understands. We can talk about a lot of things—like boys, what dress to wear, or how to kiss—and she really knows how I feel. I could tell her things I couldn't tell anyone else."

Peer Shock

Moving from childhood through adolescence is in many ways like moving from one culture into another. Changes in behaviors, customs, taboos, and relationships can bring surprises along with the adjustments. This is what David Elkind calls *peer shock.*[24]

Childhood relationships are determined by who lives nearby or has the play equipment. Among teenagers, however, belonging to the group is determined by different criteria. Social standing, popularity, ethnic background, and economic resources can cause some former playmates to feel left out and rejected.

Elkind identifies three forms of peer shock: *exclusion, betrayal,* and *disillusion. Exclusion* comes when adolescents begin to base their acceptance on social standing or other exclusive standards. Childhood friends are shocked when they move into junior high or middle school and sense rejection from the friend down the street because he now runs with a different group.

Betrayal is experienced because friendships are more complex than childhood friendships. Children generally base their friendships around cooperation and activities. Teenagers base their friendships around trust and loyalty as well as the cooperation of childhood. During the teenage years, the young person discovers the sting of friends who misuse and abuse this trust and loyalty or who exploit this trust and loyalty for personal advantage.

Disillusion strikes teenagers when they become attracted to the opposite sex. Children tend to view members of the opposite sex as rivals, but puberty changes this view. Teenage boys and girls begin to see members of the opposite sex as interesting to look at and talk about. Teenagers idealize other teenagers in their "crushes" and see them as perfect in every way. These crushes can be short lived. Disillusionment and disappointment set in when adolescents realize their romantic ideals and other close friends are mere humans and are not really perfect.

17

Mental Development of Adolescents

The changes in physical appearance during adolescence are the most noticeable, and adults may think these changes create the greatest adjustments teenagers have to make. However, the changes in mental processes are just as dramatic and may create even greater challenges than physical growth.

Adolescents develop the ability to think on a higher level, what David Elkind calls "thinking in a new key."[25]

Formal Operational Thinking

The Swiss psychologist Jean Piaget has outlined four stages of mental development:[26]

- Sensorimotor stage—birth to eighteen months
- Preoperational stage—eighteen months to seven years
- Concrete operations stage—seven to twelve years
- Formal operations stage—twelve years upward

In the sensorimotor stage the infant learns to respond to the persons and objects around him. He learns to grasp objects, move around, and adjust to the world around. As language develops, the preschooler moves into the preoperational stage of development. He can learn to manipulate meanings as well as objects. He can deal with objects as symbols for other objects. For example, a block of wood can represent a car or a doll can represent a baby.

The stage of concrete operations brings impressive mental growth to the school-age child. During this stage, thoughts become internalized and the child learns to reason and think in relational terms. He can group objects into categories and classes and do logical thinking on an elementary level. However, this reasoning is always tied to real objects and people. The child can only deal with those things with which he or she has had direct personal experience.

Formal operational thinking is a giant step in mental development for the adolescent. The adolescent is able to deal not just with the immediate and real but with the possible. Problem solving is enhanced because the teenager is able to approach a problem by imagining all the possible solutions and thinking through the consequences of each possibility. In the game of twenty questions, for example, teenagers and children approach the challenge in different ways. Teenagers are more likely to ask questions that define the object into increasingly narrower categories. ("Is it alive? Is it an animal?") In contrast, the younger child is more likely to simply ask a series of questions that are just guesses. ("Is it a bird? Is it a fish?")

Intelligence in adolescence is not just an increase in quantity but an increase in quality of thinking. Teenagers do not simply know *more* than children. They are able to *do more* with what they know. They think in a new key.

Understanding How Teenagers Think

Adolescents begin to think in abstract terms. They can manipulate thoughts concerning the world of the possible as well as the world of the real. They can generalize, state broad truths for all humankind, and deal with fantastic and absurd possibilities. This may be one reason fantasy games are so popular with teenagers.

New ways of thinking bring problems as well as potential. The new mental muscles are like the new physical muscles that create clumsiness and awkwardness. Teenagers stumble and fall mentally as well as physically. Adults can benefit from knowing some of the stumbling blocks that accompany the mental growth of teenagers.

Mental Overload

Formal operations is a giant step forward in mental growth. The young teenager finds herself flooded with thoughts, options, and possibilities. Problems do not always have one easy solution. Words and actions can have more than one meaning. Friends do not always mean what they say.

The young person begins to ask, "What did he mean by that?" When a teacher asks a question, the youth may think, *What I am thinking sounds too simple. There must be a deeper answer to that.* As a result, the teenager's mind sometimes freezes up, not because he cannot think of anything to say, but because he is thinking of too many things to say. This is what David Elkind calls *pseudostupidity.*[27]

We all have the tendency at times to approach subjects at a more complex level than is necessary. We sometimes suspect complex, devious motives in what people say or do when in reality the actions are simple and straightforward. For example, a youth leader asks the class a simple question, and everyone stares blankly. They appear to be stupid, when in fact they may be reeling with possible answers but are afraid that what they are thinking is far too simple. The adolescent mind has locked up, not because the teenager is stupid, but because he or she is smarter than ever before and has not yet learned to handle these new mental muscles.

Critical Idealism

Formal operational thinking brings greater powers of logic and deduction. It also brings the ability to think in broad, abstract, general terms. This youthful idealism is refreshing until it collides with parental pragmatism. Teenagers want to know "why" and will not settle for "because I told you so."

Every parent knows that a small child learning to count will demonstrate the ability to count to a thousand at the slightest invitation. The child wants to practice her new ability with mathematics. As a teenager, she wants to practice her new mental capacities by arguing with mom or dad about many things, with or without an invitation to practice her new logical prowess. Many family arguments are really practice sessions for adolescent logic.

Teenagers can see problems and verbalize solutions for all humankind in broad, idealistic terms. Adults tend to see problems pragmatically, realizing from their own experiences that solutions take actions as well as words. The worlds of teenagers and adults sometimes clash when teenagers, because of their new mental capacities, see the world in idealistic terms and adults, because of their base of experiences, see the world in terms of the practical.

Egocentricity

Formal operational thinking also means that the young person is able to think about thinking. Children tend to think about actions, but teenagers increasingly think about thinking. As a result, they begin to become very self-conscious of their physical shape, social relationships, and thinking processes. They become self-centered in many ways.

Teenagers assume everyone around them is interested in them and what they are thinking. This assumption is what David Elkind calls the *imaginary audience*.[28] We all have felt the glare of everyone around us when we stumble and fall in public or drop a plate of food in a crowded restaurant. We feel sure everyone is thinking, *What a clumsy person!* In fact, some probably turned and looked and then went about their business. At that moment we felt an imaginary audience staring relentlessly at us.

What adults feel *sometimes* is what teenagers feel *almost all the time*. Because they are thinking about what people are thinking, they become conscious of their own thoughts and the thoughts of others. This leads to two sticky problems for teenagers.

First, they assume everyone is concerned about the same things they are. The young teenager who is anxious about physical development may think, *My nose is too big.* He also thinks, *Everyone thinks my nose is too big!* This creates even more self-consciousness and the teenager extends his self-centeredness to all areas of life.

The second problem is almost opposite from the first. As teenagers try to understand the changes in their lives, they feel their situation is unique. One example is the daughter who says, "No one understands how much we are in love!" The young person believes she is the first person in the history of the world to experience these feelings, and no one can understand how deeply they care, how wonderfully they love each other, how hurt they have been, or how ashamed they are for mistakes made.

Clumsy Decision Making

Adolescence is a time for learning how to make decisions. Teenagers often want to make their own decisions as a sign of maturity but have trouble making good decisions. The new mental muscles provide the ability to think of many options, and these options create a tangled web of decisions. For example, a teenager may think she knows what she will order at her favorite fast-food restaurant. However, she will study the menu at some length because there are too many choices of new foods.

Teenagers sometimes make choices that seem bizarre. Adults have established some guidelines or strategies for making decisions, but teenagers are still relying on their new mental muscles and their new emotional experiences. Their mood swings can also color their decisions.

Adolescents behave in risk-taking, dangerous ways because they have not learned how to make decisions. They assume that bad things will happen to others, but not to them. "Others will get pregnant, but not me." "Others will get hooked on drugs, but not me." "Others may have a wreck and be killed driving 100 miles an hour, but not me." These dangerous assumptions grow out of mistaken adolescent feelings that they are somehow above the ordinary and protected from the normal problems that affect others.

Apparent Hypocrisy

Hypocrisy happens when words and actions do not match. The stage of formal operational thinking means adolescents can state broad general truths for all humankind but they fail to match these broad general idealisms with specific actions.

Our teenage daughter states loudly and clearly that it is wrong for anyone (especially her older brother) to go into someone's room and take things that do not belong to him. That same daughter, however, walks into her mother's room and chooses dresses, jewelry, and accessories to wear without asking for permission. Imagine how hypocritical this looked when my wife discovered a friend of our daughter's wearing a blouse that belonged to my wife!

Teenagers almost feel that stating something is the same thing as doing it. Adults realize that idealisms must be fleshed out with work and effort. When a youth group from Texas wants to take a trip to Hawaii, the adults respond by talking about the cost, logistics, and practical aspects of the venture. A healthy dose of idealism is refreshing for youth and adults, but adults must guide teenagers to realize the practical applications of their words.

18

Spiritual Development and Faith Formation

Adolescents grow and develop in many ways—physically, mentally, socially, and emotionally. They change in their relationships with friends and family members. They also experience changes in their spiritual lives that affect their relationships with God, others, and their own self-esteem.

Adolescent Development and Spiritual Growth

Teenagers are "on the way" toward maturity in many areas of life, including their spiritual development. We may want to help youth become mature believers in God, but we must remember they are still growing spiritually as well as physically, mentally, socially, and emotionally. They cannot be mature Christians as teenagers any more than they can be mature adults as teenagers.

This does not excuse adults and youth from the responsibilities of guiding and growing in spiritual maturity. Just as youth must learn to cope with changing social relationships, emotional urges, and thinking processes, they must also learn to deal with the implications of these changes for their spiritual growth.

Physical development is a major change of adolescence. Teenagers grow rapidly. They look at their faces and bodies in the mirror each day and wonder about the changes taking place inside them. "Am I normal?" "When will I ever start growing?" "When will I ever stop growing?"

Many teenagers have an idealized picture of the perfect body. When they compare themselves to this image, they fall pitifully short. It is a short leap to blaming God for the "mistakes" in their physical shape. Teenagers who think they are unattractive to everyone else may find it hard to believe that God loves them unconditionally.

Social and emotional growth carries a load of doubts and fears about one's relationship with God. A teenager who feels unsure of himself in a crowd may project those same feelings toward God. When peers reject a teenager's friendship, can God's rejection be far behind? Arguments and strained relationships with parents can color the relationship the teenager has with the same God of his or her mom and dad.

New temptations entice teenagers. Sexual and social awareness provide temptations that make young people doubt their relationship with God. "If I were a real Christian, would I be tempted like this?" "How can God love me when I think such dirty thoughts?"

Mental development opens up new ways of thinking about the familiar stories of childhood. Youth who have grown up in church discover the Bible stories of childhood have deeper meanings. The new mental muscles of adolescence cause many to question and probe the truths they once accepted so easily.

The faith of mom and dad is no longer sufficient. Faith must become personal. Parents and youth leaders can help youth by allowing—even encouraging—them to question, probe, and search for their own answers to matters of faith. When challenged or questioned about their belief in God, only those who have personally invested themselves in the search for faith will be able to "make a defense to everyone who asks you to give an account for the hope that is in you" (1 Pet. 3:15).

Faith Development Theory

Several theories of faith development are in vogue today. One of the most influential is that of James Fowler who describes six stages of human faith.[29] These stages are sequential and common to all human beings. Fowler is interested in faith as a way all humans see ourselves, other people, and the ultimate values and meanings of life. It is not necessarily centered on content nor seen as a particular Christian activity. A Christian, Marxist, and Hindu, for example, could all be at the same stage of faith development.

Fowler contends that there are predictable stages of faith development that closely parallel other stages of life. The content of the faith may differ and change, but the structure and style will always be according to the six stages. Some people may only reach stage 3, while others may reach stage 6. The route to the higher stages will be the same.

Fowler's six stages are:
1. Intuitive-Projective Faith (early childhood)
2. Mythical-Literal Faith (ages six to twelve)
3. Synthetic-Conventional Faith (ages twelve and beyond)
4. Individuative-Reflective Faith (early adulthood and beyond)
5. Conjunctive Faith (mid-life and beyond)

6. Universalizing Faith (mid-life and beyond)

Fowler's third stage, "synthetic-conventional," is the stage associated with most adolescents. This stage begins when a person is able to reflect on his own thinking. It is synthetic in the sense that the person seeks to pull beliefs and self-image together. It is called conventional because it is concerned with the expectations and judgments of others. It is the way adolescents make order out of life and conform to a group of significant others. God is seen as one's best friend and an extension of interpersonal relationships.

Some teenagers may still be in stage 2, "mythical-literal" faith. This is characterized by magical qualities shaped by extremely literal understanding. God is seen as an old man with a white beard sitting on top of the world. Adults can help these youth move to a more mature faith by employing their new mental development.

During later adolescence, the teen may move into stage 4, "individuative-reflective" faith. This involves stepping back and taking a critical, reflective look at one's faith. To some, this may look like rebellion and rejection of faith. However, it may be important in the process of faith development.

Saving Faith

"For by grace you have been saved through faith; and that not of yourselves, it is the gift of God" (Eph. 2:8). Theories of faith development help us understand the processes of faith formation but do little to help us understand the saving relationship with God.

What does it mean to believe? Is it a mental process or acceptance of authoritative truth? Daniel Aleshire proposes an important question regarding these two definitions of belief, "Is the belief that leads to salvation a belief *in* Jesus Christ—trusting him as Savior and Lord? Or is it a belief *that* Jesus is the Son of God, was crucified, buried, and rose on the third day?"[30]

The Bible states that even the demons believe *that* Jesus is the Son of God and resurrected Lord (Jas. 2:19). But demons are not repentant, do not have trust and confidence in Christ, and have no saving faith in Christ. Clearly, both types of faith are part of the Christian experience, but the faith that saves is believing *in* Jesus Christ.

Aleshire makes three statements describing saving faith.[31] He asserts that even if youth know the Scriptures backward and forward but do not trust Christ as Savior and Lord, they have not received saving faith.[32]

A Matter of the Heart

Youth must learn to love and be loved by God. They must channel their new emotions in appropriate ways toward loving God, other people, and themselves.

Ideas or Propositions Which Are True

After youth learn to believe *in* they learn to believe *that*. Paul writes, "That if you confess with your mouth Jesus as Lord, and believe in your heart that God raised Him from the dead, you shall be saved; for with the heart man believes, resulting in righteousness, and with the mouth he confesses, resulting in salvation" (Rom. 10:9-10). Saving faith means we affirm that Jesus Christ is real, the Son of God, and the Lord.

More Than Feeling and Thinking

It acts! While affirming that belief is essential to salvation, James says, "But prove yourselves doers of the word, and not merely hearers who delude themselves" (Jas. 1:22). Saving faith means putting beliefs into action in daily living.

Saving faith involves personal decisions which often come into focus during the teenage years. These decisions come as responses to the call to know Christ as Savior and Lord, to live lives holy and acceptable to God, and to be sensitive to a call to Christian vocations.

Profession of faith in God is an important decision that may come during the teenage years. If a teen made this decision earlier, he may have doubts or questions about salvation during the adolescent years. New temptations, new thinking potentials, and a search for identity lead the youth to reevaluate earlier decisions made on childhood faith.

Sometimes youth who question an earlier decision are experiencing conviction for the first time. Perhaps they made a decision because a friend did or they were coerced into a premature decision. They made their decision because of others, not because of the convicting power of sin and God's promise of a change of heart and life.

On the other hand, youth who question their earlier profession of faith may have had an authentic experience of repentance and salvation. The emerging social, sexual, and mental development of teenagers leads to new temptations . Some teenagers misinterpret guilt as the need for salvation again. They think that true Christians do not experience the temptations they now face. Adults need to guide youth into a deeper understanding of the forgiving grace and mercy of God.

Still other teenagers gain a deeper understanding of the meaning of Christianity. As the stories of the Bible take on deeper significance and they understand the commitment required to be a consistent follower of Christ, they realize they did not know these things when they made an earlier commitment of faith. They may wonder, *If that is true, then how could I have been a Christian before now?* New understandings do not weaken earlier commitments authentically made on the understanding of that period of life.

Many youth make decisions about vocation, marriage, and further education during the teenage years. Some youth may make commitments to church-related vocations. Youth leaders can faithfully guide youth to make those decisions in conscious recognition of the prompting of God in their lives.

Youth frequently struggle with their relationship with God. The search for identity and self-acceptance causes them to question and doubt their own worth. Some youth project these doubts to their own acceptance of God's love. Youth may ask, "If I don't like myself and don't think my friends like me, how can God possibly like me?" A youth who has just had an argument with his parents will have a hard time feeling loved and protected by God.

Questions about salvation and acceptance may be based on emotions rather than biblical truths. Adults should not try to manipulate youth into making decisions based on guilt or fear. Statements such as, "Unless you are absolutely sure at this moment that you would go to heaven if you die, then you're not saved," are inappropriate for teenagers. Teenagers are often not *absolutely* sure of *anything*, especially their own feelings and emotions. Adults need to choose their words carefully and make sure youth understand what the words mean.

Youth can be guided to base their salvation on biblical truth and the grace and mercy of God rather than on personal works or fleeting emotions. John 10:27-29 clearly teaches that salvation is what God does and eternal life is a gift. Security comes from God and is not earned by us. Even King David, whom God identified as, "a man after His own heart" (1 Sam. 13:14), committed a terrible sin (2 Sam. 11), repented (Ps. 51), and was forgiven (Ps. 32). Decisions of rededication may be appropriate for teenagers as they seek to live holy lives and move toward deeper understandings of saving faith.

19

Communicating with Youth

The pastor sat at the table in my doctoral seminar and confessed, "I prepare sermons every week without a lot of problems. However, when I had to preach at youth camp last summer, I was scared to death!"

The mother of a teenage girl could barely hold back the tears as she asked, "How can I get through to my daughter? It seems like we never talk anymore."

Youth leaders, parents, and anyone who speaks to teenagers have to face the issue of communication with youth. Merton and Irene Strommen report a desire in youth and parents alike for better communication in the home.[33] The ability to communicate well with teenagers is also an important skill for youth leaders. This section explores the development of these two areas of communication with youth.

Communication Skills for Parents

If both parents and youth want to communicate with each other, why is communication in the home so hard? Why do they not communicate more? Part of youth ministry involves teaching parents and youth to communicate.

A nationwide study of young adolescents and their parents revealed four reasons why the two groups do not communicate well. First, most parents and teenagers lack the *skills* necessary for good communication. Second, they do not use the kind of *at-home diplomacy* that would be used in dealing with friends or acquaintances. Third, there usually is not the kind of *trigger event* that opens up a conversation when both parties are in the mood to discuss a topic. When the teenager comes home two hours after curfew, that is not the time to discuss the topic of curfews in general. Finally, they lack the *courage* to deal with issues. It takes a great deal of emotional energy to begin discussing moral issues. Harsh words can be said, egos can be bruised, and walls can be thrown up in emotionally charged conversations. It takes courage to launch into a conversation with so much at stake.[34]

Communication skills for parents can be learned and developed. Here are some ideas for aiding the communication process between parents and their teens. Many of the principles also apply to communication between youth leaders, youth ministers, and youth.

Understanding the Need for Independence

Adolescents want freedom. They are in the process of becoming independent adults, capable of making decisions without relying on parents. Roland Martinson says, "An adolescent wants freedom. She wants to go her own way, choose her own friends, and have her own thoughts. She holds things inside. She has secrets."[35]

Teenagers may express their desire for independence by holding back information, thoughts, or feelings from parents. Arguing, disagreeing, and silence are not always signs of rebellion. They may simply be ways to show independence. Parents who recognize this can avoid arguments by looking for healthy ways for their teenagers to make decisions and allowing them some times for privacy.

Teenagers are preoccupied with themselves, trying to sort through the radical changes happening to their bodies, minds, and emotions. They tend to be quite self-conscious. Anything that could be interpreted as a correction or criticism is a sting to the ego. Parents should be sensitive to this tendency and not interpret it only as, "Leave me alone!"

Working on Listening Skills

Adolescents generally do not have good verbal skills. They cannot easily describe their feelings and thoughts. Parents can help their teens by being patient and actively listening.

Adults often think more about what they are going to *say* than about what the other person is *saying*. When a teenager is saying something, the parent may be concentrating on how he or she will respond. We can improve our listening skills by doing the following.

First, focus on the teen. Too often we listen with one ear while trying to hear the television with the other. Dad may be trying to finish a project at the moment his teen wants to talk. Parents should give their teen attention, even if it means missing part of the game.

Second, clarify what the teen is saying. This means Mom repeats to the teen what she heard her say. If her daughter complains about a teacher who is unfair, Mom may say, "It sounds like you think she's treating people unfairly." This does not mean Mom agrees or disagrees. It just communicates that Mom heard the message and wants her to continue.

Third, listen for feelings. Look for more than the content of the words the teenager says. Look for the feelings behind the words. Try to identify those feelings and repeat those to your teen. When hisson wants to drop a class because the teacher has favorites, Dad may say, "Do you feel like he ignores you sometimes?" Or, "How do you feel about . . . ?" This may not be the correct feeling, but it helps sort out feelings and put the correct ones into words.

Fourth, watch for body language. Eyes, arms, facial expressions, and other nonverbal messages often say as much as the words ateen speaks. One suggestion that helps is to mirror the actions of teens and then help them open up and relax. For example, if a youth has her arms crossed, her legs crossed, and is very tense, begin by crossing your arms and legs like her. Then, uncross your arms and let them rest in your lap. Very often, she will begin to follow your model and relax in her body language as well as her conversation.

Fifth, respond carefully. Too often we try to continue the conversation by asking questions like a prosecuting lawyer. Or, we respond with criticism or suggestion on how he should have handled the situation. Avoid judgmental responses and drill instructor questions. Encourage your teens to think through possible solutions for themselves and offer suggestions when you are invited. Try to think of the youth as a friend who has confided in you with a problem. You would not answer a friend by saying, "Well! I knew that would happen if you didn't change! If you had just listened to me you wouldn't be in this mess!"

Finally, delay the conversation when emotions are too high. It is better to postpone a conversation when you are not ready to listen effectively. Allow the emotions to cool, and you will have a better chance at a productive conversation. This does not imply that we should avoid confronting issues. It simply means that communication is better than confrontation.

Choosing the Right Place to Talk

Where is the right place to talk? It can be anyplace both parties feel comfortable talking! Communication is easier when you enter a teen's world in a casual, friendly way. Sitting on the floor may be better than sitting on the couch in the living room. Avoid talking seriously too soon. Begin the conversation lightly, finding common interests to discuss. Allow time to get in the mood of talking.

Some of the best times for our family talks have been late at night around the kitchen table. Sitting in our pajamas and eating a late night snack, we have talked through many issues that needed to be discussed. Curfews have been negotiated, grades discussed, allowances adjusted, and many of the knotty problems of parent-teen relationships were resolved over a bowl of popcorn or a cup of hot chocolate.

Other locations for good communication for our family have been the bedrooms. When our son and daughter were both younger they enjoyed lying across our bed and talking. As they grew older my wife or I would often slip into their rooms after the lights were off and talk quietly about the things of life. Sometimes, as I would sit beside the bed of my teenage son in the darkness, we could talk about things that were difficult to face in the bright lights of day. Many times he would put an arm around my neck and we would hug. Communication was profound without even a word being spoken.

Spending Time Together

For teenagers, love is spelled T-I-M-E. Quality time is important, but it usually comes in the midst of a quantity of time. Good communication cannot be programmed to happen when we plan for it. The best stance for parents to help communication is to spend time with their teens.

One of the toughest problems facing families today is finding time to be together. Schedules, routines, and demands on our time tend to pull families apart rather than help them spend time together. Even church activities, though worthy and important, can make it difficult for families to be together.

Parents and youth must take the initiative and find times to be together. Mealtimes are not always easy to schedule, but families can be creative in finding ways to get together for meals. Plan some meals during the week for the family to eat together, even if it is at a fast-food restaurant.

Family rituals, holidays, vacations, and celebrations are important times to bring parents and youth closer. Informal, unstructured times make it easier to overcome the barriers to communication. Playing basketball, going on a picnic, going to a shopping mall, or working on a project opens up opportunities for discussion.

Being Honest and Open

Sometimes the struggle toward independence for adolescents causes them to be critical toward their parents. They look for the most minute fault and use it in the next argument. Parents often respond by trying to hide or excuse their own shortcomings.

The most troubling problems for parents come when they see their teens struggling with an issue *they* never resolved. Problems with grades, sexuality, friends, dating, or parental relationships are stickiest when the parent had the same problem as a teenager. They are especially troublesome if the parent never worked through the issue with his own parents. Those problems can be difficult to address in honest, open ways.

Problems may hit close to home, and parents can feel torn between shock, disappointment, and compassion. Good communication will keep the avenues open for future discussion. Strommen and Strommen say,

> When young people learn their parents are committed to open discussion carried on in a spirit of humility, they will grow in their ability to share personal experiences and ideas. It is in this kind of atmosphere also that the strength of a parent's faith comes through to a child, as, for instance, in a time of great stress.[36]

Parents must learn to put aside fears of past figures, if they are to communicate openly with their teens. It is a risk that calls for courage and confidence. It is a risk that is worth the benefit of better parent-teen communication.

Communication Skills for Youth Leaders

Many of the same skills needed by parents for good communication with teens can also be used by youth leaders. There are some special skills needed, however, for those who speak to groups of youth. The following are some suggestions for effective communication with a youth audience.

Know the Audience

I spend a lot of time visiting schools and other places where youth gather. A school assembly program is a fascinating learning experience. The audience is usually more interesting than the program on the stage! Potential speakers will do well to become observers of the youth scene to discover audience reactions, length of attention span, and topics of interest to youth today.

An understanding of the audience will help speakers know how to pace their talk and hold the attention of the group. Younger youth have a short attention span. Older youth try hard to look uninterested, especially if they believe this impresses the boy or girl sitting near them.

Illustrations and applications are easier if the speaker knows the group. Ideally, the speaker should know personal interests and needs of individuals. This is not always possible, but general illustrations appropriate for the age group can still be used.

Make the Content Relational

Most sermons do not include illustrations related to youth. When illustrations about youth are used, they are most often negative illustrations (teenage pregnancy, drug abuse, peer pressure, rebellion, and so forth). Seek ways to personalize messages by using illustrations drawn from the lives of teenagers today.

Jesus used stories and illustrations familiar to His audiences. When listeners hear a point communicated through a story that could have happened that day at school, they pay attention.

Develop Good Speaking Skills

Put forth the effort in planning and sharpening your message. Good speaking rarely comes without good preparation.

Select a topic. This normally comes from a passage of Scripture or an issue facing the group. Spend appropriate time studying the biblical content and locating cross references and illustrations from the Bible.

Write a summary sentence that states the main idea. Follow this by writing some statements about why this is important to the youth in the group. Then outline your message with two to four major points. For each point, think of an illustration and an application. Interesting facts from encyclopedias or reference books add spice to the topics or major points in your talk.

Begin with a story or humorous illustration to introduce the topic. This will gain attention and make the audience want to hear more. Give them a taste of the outcome of the message with the first illustration.

Plan for the message to move smoothly toward the conclusion. Keep it simple and straightforward. Youth are not impressed by academic language and complex logic. A well-planned, lively message will make a better impression on adolescents. The conclusion should restate the main point. It should summarize the applications and point toward any decisions that might need to be made. An illustration, hymn text, or poem can often be effective in driving home the main point.

Observe good speakers and the things to which youth are responsive. Discern the patterns, mannerisms, and styles of speakers who are effective communicators. Adapt these to your own style and personality. Do not attempt to use the slang or dress of the teenagers in order to gain their attention. Nothing looks more ridiculous than an overgrown adolescent trying to communicate in words that went out of date last week! Warmth and love for teenagers will come through if you are sincere.

Keep a Healthy Sense of Humor

Some of the best advice I ever heard was from my teacher, Dr. Phil Briggs, "Take your message very seriously, but don't take yourself too seriously." Adults who feel comfortable enough to use humor can build bridges between themselves and the listeners. A stilted, formal style builds walls that keep many teenagers from hearing the message.

Humor can be a powerful tool if used correctly. We do not want to be seen as stand-up comedians but as speakers of the truth. Make sure the humor is appropriate, understandable to the age group, and not destructive or degrading. Never use sarcasm or ridicule. The price of riddled self-esteem is not worth the few moments of laughter from the audience.

Speak Through the Power of the Holy Spirit

Many of these suggestions apply to speakers in any group, secular or Christian. The primary difference for Christian speakers is the role of the Holy Spirit.

If we are to be authentic servants of God, communicating the message of hope to a lost world, we must draw our strength and direction through the working of the Holy Spirit. Our message must grow out of a life centered on and submissive to God's will. Our relationship with Christ must be in order and pleasing to God.

Prayer is an essential element in communicating with youth. It is through communication with God that we know His heart and desire. Through prayer we can be filled with the power and insight to speak the truth. When we are sensitive to the Holy Spirit, our cups will be filled with the living water of salvation and hope.

We may not all be powerful speakers, able to sway a crowd with elegance and persuasion. But we can make an impact through a message that is authentic and energized with the Spirit of God. In our own strength we might do little to change the course of history. But, as Paul says, "My message and my preaching were not in persuasive words of wisdom, but in demonstration of the Spirit and of power, that your faith should not rest on the wisdom of men, but on the power of God" (1 Cor. 2:45).

20

Guiding Vocational Decisions

Critical Decisions

Youth make critical decision during their high school years. As they struggle with who they are, they also make choices about what they will do: what to study in school, where to go to college, what to be, who to marry, and other decisions.

Even before high school, some of these concerns begin to focus as the youth face choices they will make during the high school years. Strommen and Strommen report that one of the top ten worries for young adolescents is not being able to "get a job when I am older."[37] This worry ranks higher for ninth graders than for other young adolescents in the study.

High school students often choose their courses based on whether or not they plan to attend college or which college they plan to attend. These decisions can come as early as the eighth grade students decide about registering for different levels of English, algebra, and science. I find it distressing that these young adolescents have to make choices about "accelerated" courses, "college-prep" tracks, or "vocational training" programs with little or no preparation.

Parents and youth often choose the same values as life goals. A study of young adolescents and their parents revealed several items of interest. The two life goals most important to young adolescents are "to have a happy family life" and "to get a good job when I am older." The two items that increase most as young adolescents approach high school are "to make my own decisions" and "to do something important with my life."[38]

Vocational decisions become increasingly important as the teenager moves into and through the high school years. Studies show that parents can be a teenager's best resource in evaluating career choices. Other youth leaders can be valuable resources in this process.

Guiding the Choices

Youth leaders can assist teenagers as they make decisions about their vocation. As youth participate in church activities, studies, and learning experiences, they gain a taste for ways of using their talents and interests.

Worship times point people toward God and offer opportunities for reflection about life goals. The call to vocation is more than a decision about what kind of work a person will do. It is about how to live life to its fullest. Vocation has to do with life goals; career has to do with earning a living. As we guide youth in decisions about college majors, careers, and the future, we must help them begin with their relationship with God and His will for their lives.

Study times help youth focus their thoughts on ways to use their minds and energies in work and service. Bible studies, discipleship groups, mission studies, and vocational seminars are a few of the ways we can help youth explore vocational choices. A career fair or special emphasis on college choices will help parents and youth make informed decisions for the future.

Youth activities and learning experiences can be a valuable resource in making career decisions. Teenagers are often uninformed about ways to use their gifts and talents in work and service. A work project or mission trip gives firsthand experience in serving others and gives youth a taste of the joy of service. Talents and gifts can be called forth in immediate application and open the doors of possible vocational choices.

Many youth have gifts and interests that could be used in Christian vocation but do not know possible avenues for preparation and service. When our son was a sophomore in high school, he took a vocational interest inventory to help determine career choice. I was shocked to see how little information was available to guide youth who may have interests in Christian vocations. The only guidance was a subparagraph under "helping professions" that listed "clergy" with only one brief paragraph of information.

The field of Christian vocations is broad and varied. Many youth have talents, gifts, and interests that could be used in serving God through these areas of ministry. Youth leaders can guide teenagers in vocational choices by following these guidelines.

Identify Strengths, Interests, and Gifts

Look for ways to enforce strengths, interests, and gifts among the youth in your group. Use these gifts in service and youth activities to allow the teenagers use their talents and energies.

Experience Success with Their Interests

A youth who enjoys art can be enlisted to help with posters and banners for the youth area. A youth who plays or sings can lead the group in music. A youth who is shy and unsure can be encouraged by working one-to-one with an adult in preparing and leading various activities.

Do Not Specialize Too Soon

Help youth explore a variety of experiences that could point toward vocational choices. If a youth has musical talents, help her also discover other areas of interests. Do not let youth label themselves according to interests or specialties too soon and shut off the possibilities of other avenues of service.

See Vocation as More Than a Job

When we ask, "What do you want to do when you grow up?" we limit vocation to a method of earning a living. Studies show that youth tend to choose jobs with high incomes. If we focus only on *job* choice, the logical choice may be the most materialistic career. God calls us to higher goals in life. Teenagers are looking for meaningful ways to give themselves in worthy causes. They will respond to a challenge if we help them see vocation as a way to invest their lives in higher callings. Then the way we earn our living becomes part of the broader choice of a vocation for life.

21

Involving Youth in Leadership

Several generations ago, concerned church members talked about their young people as the "church of tomorrow." They would plan activities (mostly after-church fellowships, parties, banquets, and trips) for the youth to hold their attention and keep them involved.

In time, churches began hiring youth directors to lead their youth programs. The activities were done *for* the youth by concerned adult church members. Neither approach is effective.

A church I once served as youth minister had a tradition of giving the youth a spring banquet. The adults planned every detail, sent printed invitations, presented a fun-filled program, served the meal, and did all the decorating and cleanup. The adults were shocked when only a few of the youth attended. Only then did the adults realize that the banquet was an *adult* banquet planned *for youth*. It was not really a youth banquet.

This highlights an important philosophy of youth ministry. Ministry *with* youth is superior to ministry *to* or *for* youth. Youth respond best when they are personally involved. They participate more and feel more ownership when they have invested time and energy in the process.

Youth who are Christians are members of the body of Christ and should be involved in the work of ministry. Teenagers learn about ministry best when they are *doing* ministry not just *hearing* about it. They are not just the church of tomorrow; they are the church *today*.

Jesus illustrated this principle on the last night alone with His disciples (John 13). He had been teaching them the principles of ministry for three years as they traveled together. However, the twelve still did not understand the servant model of leadership. Jesus picked up a towel and wash basin, assumed the role of a servant, and began to wash the feet of the disciples. Their responses were shock and disbelief. Jesus said they must be involved in ministry ("wash one another's feet") if they were to truly follow His example (vv. 12-17).

Mark Senter underlines the importance of involving youth in leadership if a youth ministry is to be effective. He states, "Student ownership of youth ministry guided by respected Christian adults is essential for the ministry to remain healthy."[39]

We have often observed Youth Week as a time to teach youth leadership and service. However, youth should learn about service and ministry all year. There are ways to involve youth in leadership in visible and behind-the-scenes roles throughout the year.

Visible Leadership Roles

Youth can assume leadership roles in the learning groups at church each week. Shared leadership in a discipleship group allows youth to plan and lead units of study. Serving as officers in Sunday School classes, missions education groups, or music groups allows them to exercise leadership gifts and develop skills in ministry.

Youth can participate in corporate worship. Leading prayers during worship, singing and performing, serving as ushers, making announcements, and sharing a testimony are ways youth can be visible leaders before the church gathered for worship.

Youth can be involved in leading children's groups in various activities. Leading Bible clubs, helping with Vacation Bible School, leading children's mission activities, helping with children's choirs, and assisting with preschoolers during worship services are some ways youth can serve.

Youth can also serve in visible ways in youth activities. Speaking at a youth group meeting, leading activities on retreats, planning and organizing youth activities, and leading at a youth fellowship allow youth to be involved in leadership. .

Youth Week is an effective way to highlight the youth of a church and develop leadership skills. As youth plan and lead in worship services, teach classes, and participate with various church leaders, they learn the joy of service in leadership.

Behind the Scene Roles

Leadership is more than one person in a visible leadership role. It also involves service in quieter, less noticeable ways. Youth who are shy or less confident may respond better to leadership roles outside the glare of the spotlight.

Youth can be enlisted to help adults plan and prepare for study sessions. An adult leader of a Bible study class could invite one of the class members to offer suggestions for teaching the next session of study. The youth will enjoy the taste of leadership without being thrust into the spotlight too soon.

Youth can also lead by preparing a room for an event. They can gather and hand out supplies, arrange the furniture, and hang posters and banners. Lighting and sound equipment is often needed for youth meetings. A youth may be fascinated by the equipment and enjoy the responsibility of operating it.

Puppet teams are visible means of communication, but it is easier to be "invisible" behind the curtain of a puppet stage. I saw a very shy young man blossom into an effective leader when he learned to perform on a puppet team. He discovered hidden talents that gave him a sense of joy and fulfillment. He now serves on the staff of a large church helping other youth discover and utilize their talents and gifts.

Basic Decision-Making Roles

Youth can and should be involved in significant decision-making roles. Many churches include at least one youth representative on each major church committee. This signals confidence and trust on the part of the congregation. Youth sense a feeling of ownership and acceptance as they work together with adults on common projects. Their comments become "our church" and "my youth group" rather than "that church" and "that youth group."

A youth ministry council is an effective way to involve youth in decision-making roles related to the total youth ministry. Representative youth, key volunteer youth leaders, and representative parents make up the youth ministry council. This group can help shape the total youth ministry of the church and provide valuable feedback for youth leaders as they plan and lead various youth programs.

Youth can assist in planning and leading youth events sponsored by the youth ministry council or various classes and groups in the church. Teenagers should be involved in the decision processes whenever possible.

Youth are dreamers and may suggest impossible events or goals for the youth group. As they are involved in carrying out the plans they make, they experience the practical aspects of seeing a project through to completion. Responsibility is a valuable by-product when youth are held accountable for carrying out the plans they make. Youth leaders should emphasize the responsibility youth have to carry out their plans. This ensures better participation at youth events, because there is built-in investment by the teenagers. Adults can work *with* youth, rather than *for* youth, to help them sense that youth ministry really is the church's ministry with youth.

22

Peer Ministry

Importance of Friends

A special form of leadership involves youth in ministry to their friends. During adolescence, teenagers become much more sensitive and aware of the influence of their friends. They discuss the issues surrounding them and look to friends for help in responding to the rapid changes going on in their lives.

A Search Institute study with young adolescents and their parents illustrates the growing tendency for teenagers to look to their peers for help. The following chart shows the percent of youth most likely to turn to parents for help with selected problems. The percentages decline as the adolescents move into the high school years.[40]

Percent who most likely would choose parents for help or advice . . .	5th grade	9th grade
When wondering how to handle my feelings	58	36
When some of my friends start using drugs or alcohol	45	31
When having questions about sex	57	38
When feeling guilty about something I have done	47	29

Although there is an abundance of research showing that the influence of peers does not cancel or eliminate the influence of parents on adolescents, this research does show the importance of friendship as a source of help. Teens look to their friends for help and guidance in the midst of adolescent adjustments. The potential for peer ministry is great. Aleshire says, "Churches need to seize the natural affinity youth have to other youth in their programs of youth ministry."[41]

Friends Helping Friends

When Jesus was asked to identify the greatest commandment, He said to love the Lord God with all your heart soul, mind, and strength. Then He added, "The second is this, 'You shall love your neighbor as yourself.' There is no other commandment greater than these" (Mark 12:31-32). Youth ministry should guide teenagers to put the greatest commandment into practice through Christian love and service.

Barbara Varenhorst is a pioneer in the area of peer ministry training. She established the Peer Counseling Program in the Palo Alto, California, public schools in 1970. Over the past two decades this program has been expanded and adapted for use by schools, social agencies, and churches across the United States.[42]

Varenhorst notes that adults often point to the negative effects of peer pressure. However, peers can also be positive influences in "teamwork, a listening ear, holding each other accountable, giving perspective, sharing Christian faith and so on."[43] Peer ministry training can help youth become the kind of Christian friends they would like to have.

Youth can easily be involved in leading sessions of study in Sunday School classes, discipleship training, and missions education groups. They can be involved in visiting and witnessing to their friends. They can perform music and drama with their peers. They can be actively involved in speaking to groups and in one-to-one relationships with their friends.

During a recent Wednesday night supper at our church, I sat beside a charming twelfth-grade girl from our youth group. She had some of her school books and a spiral-bound notebook on the table in front of her. As we talked she said she had to plan for the next meeting with her "little sister" at school. I discovered she met regularly with a ninth-grade girl who needed help with her school subjects and behavior. This type of approach to peer tutoring is widely used in schools in our area. It could easily be adapted to youth ministry in several ways.

Provide Training in Helping Skills

The high school my daughter attends has a "Natural Helpers" program similar to the illustration above. Students selected by teachers were enlisted to attend a weekend retreat on relational skills. They were taught how to be good listeners and how to help a friend find help with a problem.

Youth groups could use the same approach to train youth in helping skills. This is not "counselor" training in the purest sense, but it helps youth guide friends toward help in crisis situations. A weekend retreat, seminar, or series of studies could provide basic helping skills for Christian youth.

Involve Youth in Discipleship Processes

The Paul-Timothy relationship in the New Testament is a popular approach to discipleship training. However, the Barnabas-John Mark approach is a better model for youth. Paul was a teacher and related to the younger Timothy as his student. Youth do not function well as "teachers" for their peers. They do function well as "encouragers" (the Barnabas model) for peers. Barnabas was an encourager to many people, but especially to young John Mark, even when he failed and disappointed Paul on his first missionary journey (see Acts 13:13; 15:36-39).

Youth can assist adults in learning experiences with other youth, but they function best in encouraging and tutoring roles. Youth leaders should look for creative ways to involve youth with other youth in these supportive roles.

Peer support groups are used in many schools and agencies to help youth with critical problems of drug abuse, suicide, eating disorders, and sexual abuse. My wife works with teenagers in a variety of these support groups. The support and accountability these teenagers draw from these support groups is amazing.

Although few churches have such support groups, they offer an open door of ministry. Many of the youth in such groups are on the fringes of church involvement. Many are dropouts from church or have never been involved in church youth groups. They do not participate because they do not feel comfortable in churches. Their alienation keeps them from joining more traditional youth activities.

Beginning such a support group requires a measure of risk for churches. It demands a level of training beyond that received by many youth ministers and volunteer leaders. It requires a commitment to follow through with long-term ministry rather than the short-term approach often used by those who only plan a series of youth activities.

Such a commitment can proclaim the good news to hurting people in ways they have not experienced. Strommen points out that most churches have emphasized the ministries of preaching and teaching. He says, "A new ministry is needed that accents a caring approach, one that is sensitive to the hurting, the lonely, the defeated, and the overwhelmed."[44]

A Word of Caution

Youth can be trained to be good listeners and to point their friends toward help in times of need. However, there are some serious considerations for those who wish to develop a peer ministry approach. Varenhorst cautions:

> But there are problems with untrained kids giving counsel to their peers. Kids often lack adequate skills for helping others effectively. Kids struggling with their identity ("Who am I?") at times feel insecure about how to find friendship and give support. They often make mistakes and act cruelly. Their developing communication skills sometimes cause miscommunication. With the purest motives, they can easily give harmful counseling.[45]

Peer ministry can offer hope to a hurting world through the relationships of youth with their friends. With proper cautions in mind, a church can benefit from a peer ministry program.

23

Reaching Youth Outside the Church

A survey of *Seventeen* magazine readers revealed some interesting statistics. Eighty-five percent say they believe in God, with two-thirds saying God is in every person. Seventy-seven percent of the girls and 76 percent of the boys say going to church is not necessary to be close to God. Seventy-six percent of the girls and 67 percent of the boys say believing in God helps a person have hope for the future.[46]

Several studies indicate that interest in religion is important, but this interest does not always result in more church involvement. The youth who are in our churches tend to be more academically successful, emotionally stable, and socially skilled than those outside the church. The outsiders naturally feel rejected and alienated from the insiders and do not want to risk further rejection (whether perceived or real) by taking steps toward church involvement.

How can we allow this to go on? The Great Commission does not say we are to reach out only to those who are "like us" or who feel comfortable in our group. If we are to fulfill Christ's command to reach the world, we must seek creative ways to find those outside the church and share with them the message of hope and grace.

Reaching the Unreached

Some youth are outside the church because they once were involved and dropped out. Some youth drop out because of jobs or other commitments that pull them away. Others drop out because they do not find friends in the youth group. It does not take a lot of friends for a youth to feel welcome, but it does take at least one friend.

A third reason youth drop out is because parents forced them to come as children and then gave them permission to drop out when they reached the teenage years. Strangely, those parents would not think of allowing their teen to drop out of school but think nothing of letting them drop out of church.

A fourth reason some youth drop out of church is because of personal sins. They begin experimenting with drugs, sex, or something else and feel guilty when they go to church. Rather than confessing sins and receiving cleansing from God, they simply drop out of church. Others drop out because they dabble in mystical philosophies such as satanism, occult, New Age, and Eastern religions. Youth who become entangled in these philosophies which contradict the good news of Jesus Christ will find it hard to remain active in youth activities.

Finally, some youth drop out because there is little or no youth involvement in the church. Youth are expected to sit passively rather than be involved in leading, planning, and reaching out. Youth are looking for more challenge and involvement than this allows for them.

Many of the same reasons keep teenagers out of the church from the beginning. Many outsiders are overwhelmed by moral issues of our society. Drug and alcohol problems; divorce and single-parent families; dysfunctional families; physical, emotional, and sexual abuse; and social alienation flood people with problems and smother the hope from their souls. They turn away from the church—the place where they could find ultimate hope for their lives.

Troubled teenagers do not mix well with "normal" teenagers. They feel like failures and do not believe they will be anything else. Their self-defeating behaviors repel people who could offer help and hope.

Parents of healthy, well-adjusted youth—the kind we often find in church youth groups—do not like for their teenagers to associate with troubled teenagers. Youth leaders who attempt to reach outsiders often face resistance from church leaders and parents when the outsiders show up. The outsiders sense they are unwelcome and leave.

How can we overcome these obstacles and reach youth outside the church? There are no easy answers. Problems are complex and may take years to resolve. The image of the youth group or church may be distorted and will take patient efforts to make a real difference.

The following suggestions can help churches reach the outsiders. Some adaptation is certainly needed in many cases.

Build on Personal Relationships

Train leaders to be personally involved with the teenagers they lead. If youth ministry is anything, it is relational. The best-made plans and smoothest-running youth ministry will never replace the personal touch. Learn as much about the teenagers in your youth group as possible—their family situations, friends, jobs, interests, grades, abilities, fears, and so on. When enlisting volunteer leaders, make sure they understand the responsibility for relating to youth outside of their classes and groups.

Model an Inclusive Attitude

As I was planning with a group of youth, we realized that the plans we discussed included only the youth who were already actively involved in church. We had to concentrate on ways to attract those teenagers who did not attend regularly.

Some volunteer leaders may be overworked with a group too large to handle. They will not want to reach other youth, especially those who may be troublemakers. Plan for better organizational patterns. Look for creative ways to reach the unreached and make them feel welcome when they attend.

Involve Youth in Planning

Youth want to be actively involved in all facets of the ministry. They will respond best when they feel it is their activity, not just another one planned by adults.

Build a Ministry with Parents

Parents of teenagers have hopes and dreams for their sons and daughters. Input and feedback from parents are vital in youth ministry.

Parents of teenagers can also be objects of ministry. Help with parenting skills, decision making, coping skills, and fellowship with other parents can be attractive elements to parents of dropouts. A parent ministry can build a strong base of support for youth ministry.

Encourage Teenagers to Bring Friends with Them

Most teenagers have several friends at school who are not involved in church. Every youth activity, class, group, learning experience, or event can be an opportunity to bring new youth. Remind the members to bring their friends and help them feel accepted. Plan special activities designed to introduce new youth to the group and meet their special needs.

Teach with Youth in Mind

Every Bible study should be strongly flavored with "So what? So what does this have to do with me?" Help youth sense God speaking to them through the lesson.

Teach with developmental and social needs in mind. Teaching a seventh grader is different from teaching a twelfth grader. Be aware of the issues and problems facing youth today. Keep in mind the attention span, interests, fears, and concerns of the group.

Keep Good Records

This may sound cold and impersonal, but it is necessary to keep up with a growing youth group. It is too easy to lose someone in a busy youth schedule. How many came to the retreat last year? When did this person stop coming to church? How many came to the last dating and sex seminar? Good records will help you see people more than numbers and guide your efforts to reach dropouts more effectively.

Expect Problems When Outsiders Attend

Some outsiders do not know how to behave in church. They may be noisy, disruptive, and distracting. Some will smoke in the bathrooms, scar the furniture, and even vandalize property. Extra security or adult chaperons can prevent some of the problems.

The disciples tried to prevent little children from distracting Jesus as He taught, but Jesus said to let them come to Him. Many outsiders are like children in the church and will need attention and guidance.

Deal Redemptively with Youth

It is easy to label outsiders as losers and troublemakers. My heart sinks when I hear people ready to dismiss teenagers because they do not dress or behave in appropriate ways. The message of Christ is one of redemption and hope. Who is going to reach and change that youth if the church does not?

Go Where the Youth Are

It is not enough to say, "Here we are. Come and see." We must carry the message of hope to teenagers on their turf. A youth leader who shows up at the school cafeteria, ball games, choir concerts, youth hangouts, the mall, and church youth activities shows a genuine interest in their needs.

Plan Socials as Outreach Events

Social events can be more than just another party. Many youth will come to a fellowship, party, banquet, or hayride before they attend a Bible study or worship time. Use these events as magnets to attract outsiders in a casual, warm atmosphere.

Plan Outreach Bible Studies

Some youth do not feel comfortable coming to a church facility. It may be easier to have a Bible study, concert, discussion group, or youth gathering at a neutral location. Involve youth in planning and leading whenever possible and focus attention on inviting new youth to these meetings.

24

Ministry with Ethnic/Language Groups

Maria is a bright, energetic teenager who attends many of our youth group activities. She attends the same high school as many teens in our group. However, she is a member of a Hispanic language church in the neighborhood. Her parents will not allow her to attend our church. Maria and her parents talk about this problem a lot.

Maria's parents speak Spanish in the home. She and her younger brothers and sisters speak English except when speaking to their parents. At their church, the worship services and the adult Bible study classes are in Spanish. The children and youth Bible study classes are conducted in English.

The Problem

Maria, like many teenagers across the United States, lives in two worlds. Her parents are concerned about the family heritage they see slipping away daily. Maria feels more comfortable in activities with friends from school. Her parents want to maintain the family traditions and roots.

These problems are compounded when church or youth groups adopt a white, middle-class stance as the biblical norm. Ethnic or language groups of teenagers may be ignored or left to "their own churches."

The Potential

Consider the size of the populations. A recent report shows that the white population of the U.S. is 205.7 million, with blacks numbering 29.4 million and others numbering 7.5 million. The number of Hispanics in the United States has tripled over the last thirty years to a total of 18.8 million. The black population increased over the six years prior to this report by 9.8 percent. Other ethnic groups (Native Americans, Asian Americans, Alaskan natives, and Pacific Islanders) increased

45 percent during this same period. This compares to a growth rate of 4.9 percent among whites.[47]

Teenagers reflect similar trends in populations shifts. The 1980 figures with projections for 1996 in each of the three groups are shown in the following chart. The numbers represent percentages of all teenagers in the United States:[48]

	1980	1996
Blacks	13.7	15.2
Hispanics	7.5	11 to 13
Native Americans, Asians and Pacific Islanders	2.3	3.9

Most Americans live in urban areas. A dramatic shift from rural to metropolitan living took place in the last half of this century. Seventy-six percent of Americans now live in metropolitan areas as compared to only 56 percent in 1950. About 66 percent of teenagers live in metropolitan areas, with 28 percent living in cities. Among ethnic teenagers, 56 percent of black teenagers and 53 percent of Hispanic teenagers live in cities.[49]

If churches hope to be effective in ministry with youth they must become aware of the growing need for reaching and relating to ethnic and language groups. We can begin by opening the eyes of our youth to the growing numbers of teenagers from ethic and language groups. Classes and discussions about ethnic, language, cultural, and racial matters can help youth be more sensitive to the needs of these teenagers. We take the first step in relating to someone when we begin to know and understand them.

Second, we can make efforts to cross cultural barriers. We often make cultural mistakes unaware of the effects this may have on someone different from us. In visits I have made overseas, cultural differences surprised me. In some countries it is offensive to pat someone on the head or walk around with your hands in your pockets. In other countries a guest is expected to bring a gift when visiting someone's home. These differences offer depth and richness to life. Other differences such as language, color of skin, or social patterns can be considered barriers unless we work to overcome them.

A seminar or class can help youth become aware of different cultures. Inviting ethnic representatives to speak or demonstrate different clothing, foods, and language can be a fun learning experience. A missions fair at church could focus on local mission efforts to reach ethnic or language groups outside the membership.

A third way we can reach ethic or language groups is to build bridges with families. Parents who speak another language may feel uncomfortable visiting an English language church. They may project this fear to their teenagers and restrict their participation in youth group activities. A relationship with parents can often pave the way for the teenager to become involved with the youth group.

A fourth way to reach ethnic or language groups, particularly in urban areas, is to plan a ministry to meet a specific need among the teenagers. Are teenagers roaming the streets because they have nothing to do? Plan an after school recreational program to appeal to them. Is there a drop-out problem in schools? A tutoring program or English language classes could be the answer. Poverty or unemployment can be monumental problems for one church to handle. However, some things can be done, even if they seem small. A clothes closet, free rides to school, or food for hungry families can offer help in times of need.

Finally, a fellowship with a focus on ethnic or language cultures may help build bridges between the groups. Invite families to set up food and craft booths, play games from the different cultures, and sing songs from the groups represented. A casual atmosphere can do much to let Christ's love show through our differences.

Part 4
Ministry with Parents of Youth

25

Ministry with Parents of Youth

I noticed a mother with a furrowed brow approaching as we loaded the bus for the weekend retreat. Her daughter was in a small huddle with some friends around the corner. The mother started talking in short, clipped sentences, with her finger wagging in my face. I knew I was in for trouble spelled with a capital *t*.

The daughter had given her some wrong information about the retreat and activities we had planned. After the mother and I talked, she realized the retreat had a completely different purpose, and we parted on a friendly note. Apparently, the mother and daughter had been arguing about other matters, and I received the leftover frustration from an anxious parent.

Similar experiences with parents often make a youth minister gunshy about relating to parents. Youth ministry has a tradition of relating only to teenagers and those adults who plan and lead the activities. Parents, even in the present models of youth ministry, seem to be viewed as roadblocks to effective youth ministry. Parents exist only to provide money for the activities and pick up the teenagers when the bus returns from the trip. This section emphasizes the need to relate to parents, minister with them, and equip parents to be vital parts of youth ministry.

On a personal note, I am a parent of teenagers. For many years earlier, I included parents of teenagers in youth ministry in a variety of ways. When my own children became teenagers, I became personally aware of the need for ministry with parents of youth. This facet of youth ministry opens an avenue of ministry that is crying for attention. Parents of teenagers are hurting in a multitude of ways and looking for help from those with a message of hope and assurance. My hope is that youth leaders will broaden their scope of ministry to include parents as an essential element of the total picture of youth ministry.

Parents Are People, Too

There is a joke among adults. It says that when you have children you cease being yourself and become someone's mommy or daddy.

139

At school you introduce yourself to the teacher and other parents as "Clay's dad" or "Melissa's mother." At Little League ball games you are the daddy of the third baseman. You are known as the Band Boosters, the Quarterback Club, the "parents" in PTA, and the ones who take pictures at all important functions at church and school.

In a church's youth ministry, parents are the ones who bring teenagers to youth functions, sign release forms before the ski trip, and pay the fees for the youth activities. In many cases, parents are seen as the ones who produced the teenagers but now should turn them over to the youth leaders for instruction and guidance. Some youth ministers mistakenly feel that parents should stay away from the youth ministry except they need sandwiches or a large home with a swimming pool for a fellowship.

How should parents be viewed? How do we describe these adults who are called parents? What is the relationship between parents of teenagers and those who lead youth in church programs and activities?

Parents of teenagers are first of all *people*. They are more than providers of the teenagers for youth activities. They are more than those who pay for and support many of the events, activities, and programs of youth ministry. They are more than external appendages to a youth ministry. They are part of God's creation and plan for growing up in families.

Parents are an *important part of a teenager's life*. Being a parent is more than the biological process of reproduction. It involves all the emotional and social facets of life in the wonderful process of growing up together. In reasonably healthy families, parents love their children more than anyone else does. They care deeply about their spiritual, mental, physical, social, and emotional growth. Parents have deeply felt hopes and dreams for their young ones.

Teenagers return those same feelings for their parents in many ways. It is encouraging news to many people that teenagers would like to have more communication with their parents. The Search Institute study with young adolescents and their parents confirms the longing for more, not less, communication.[1] Laurence Steinberg, in his text on adolescent development, says,

> Study after study on this issue has shown that although some adolescents and their parents have serious interpersonal problems, the overwhelming majority of adolescents feel close to their parents, respect their parents' judgment, feel that their parents love and care about them, and have a lot of respect for their parents as individuals.[2]

Parents are also *people in need of ministry*. Along with the usual concerns of middle-age adults, the concern over being a good parent of their teenagers is a nagging source of worry. Strommen and Strommen say that the greatest concern of most parents is that they will fail as parents.[3]

Our society tends to place responsibility on parents for anything that goes wrong with their children. Tony Campolo responded to this view by pointing out, "God created two biologically perfect children, placed them in a perfect environment and yet both rebelled and ruined their lives. Placing guilt on parents lacks scientific validation."[4]

Parents need of ministry in several ways that relate to a church's youth ministry. They need to be understood as persons in their own right. They need help and encouragement in the challenging job of parenting children, especially through the adolescent years. Finally, they need the fellowship and nurture of peers who are struggling to know and respond to the promptings of God in their lives.

The Tasks of Mid-Life

It may seem strange to include a section on the developmental tasks of middle-age adults in a book on youth ministry, but an understanding of the life processes of parents of adolescents adds a depth and quality to youth ministry that has been missing in previous generations. Understanding parents will help the youth minister avoid taking sides on the teenagers' behalf and naively seeing parents as "the enemy."

Parents of adolescents are usually thirty to fifty years of age, the time of life called middle age. Men and women in the middle years of adulthood reach the peak of their influence upon society at the same time society makes some of its greatest demands on them. It is the time of life filled with demands and complex relationships, stemming from children who are becoming emotionally independent and aging parents who are becoming emotionally dependent on the middle-age adults. A deeper understanding of these middle-age adults as they grow in relation to their children and their own parents will provide a stance for more mature youth ministry.

Robert Havighurst lists seven developmental tasks of mid-life.[5] A brief listing of these tasks will provide a basis for understanding middle-age parents of adolescents.

Developmental Tasks of Middle Age
1. Assisting teenage children to become responsible and happy adults.
2. Achieving adult social and civic responsibility.
3. Reaching and maintaining satisfactory performance in one's occupational career.
4. Developing adult leisure-time activities.

5. Relating oneself to one's spouse as a person.
6. Accepting and adjusting to the physiological changes of middle age.
7. Adjusting to aging parents.

Ministering to the Needs of Parents

The father of one of our teenagers shared a cup of coffee with me at a break. The weather was cold, and the coffee and friendship made the day brighter. We talked about several things, including an emphasis our church was having on strengthening Christian homes. As we talked he confided that he sincerely wanted to have family devotions but did not know how to start. I realized that most of the time I encouraged parents to have family devotions but hardly ever equipped them to do it.

Help Parents with Spiritual Leadership in the Home

There are a lot of books and resources for families with children or preschoolers. Bible storybooks, magazines, songs, and picture books abound with ideas for leading family devotions when there are preschoolers or children in the family.

However, when the children reach the teens, most of the resources for spiritual growth turn toward private devotions for the teenager. There are fewer sources of ideas for *family* Bible study, worship, or discussions about the things of God. As a result, parents find it difficult to begin or maintain a consistent, family devotion time.

Youth ministers can assist parents by providing training along with encouragement in having a family devotion time. Provide materials, tapes, magazines, books, and models for having family devotions. Offer seminars, discussions, brainstorming sessions, films, or videos to equip parents for the role of spiritual leadership in the home. Both parents and teenagers will benefit.

Equip Parents for Their Parenting Role

Parenting teenagers is like no other job in the world. It bears little resemblance to being a parent of preschoolers or children. Although the relationships formed during the earlier years of childhood set the stage for the parent-teenager experience, there is no smooth continuum between the former and the latter.

Many parents find the heat has been turned up in the parent-teen relationships. The problems and challenges feel like someone has pushed the fast-forward button on a VCR. Communication alternates between silence and high volume at unpredictable times. Schedules move into the fast lane. Parents look around with puzzled expressions, wondering who suddenly changed the rules.

Youth ministers can assist parents by providing help with parenting skills. Young parents may seek help from all directions when they have a newborn baby. Many parents do not know where to find help in coping with the new demands they face as parents of teenagers.

A parent ministry designed to address the needs of parents of teenagers can be a vital part of an effective youth ministry. Regular meetings, discussion times, guest speakers, tapes, videos, seminars, and training sessions are a few of the ideas that parents of teenagers have found helpful.

Younger youth ministers should not avoid trying to help parents in this area. The key is to listen to the needs of parents, seek their input in planning topics for discussion, and involve them in setting the direction of training. It may seem difficult for single youth ministers, or those with no teenagers of their own, to help others with ideas for rearing their teenagers. Parents will appreciate the opportunity to learn better parenting skills, gain understanding of their teenagers, and exchange ideas regarding allowance, curfews, limits, and problem-solving.

Build Relationships with Parents

As a youth minister, I would spend a lot of time with youth on Sunday mornings and evenings. Before and after classes and worship times, visit and develop friendships. One day I decided to visit the classes where their parents met. I went to the middle-adult department and discovered a wonderful array of new relationships. I believe the youth ministry broadened and gained new depth as a result of the relationships that developed from spending more time with the parents of teenagers in our youth group.

New understandings of parent-teen relationships, the interests of the youth in the group, and the struggles and joys of parents grew out of the times I spent with the adults who were the youth parents. A few minutes spent in fellowship or greeting parents as they arrive at church can blossom into bonds of trust and mutual support for the entire youth ministry.

Youth ministers can assist parents by thoughtful acts and times spent with them in fellowship and discussion. Birthday cards or notes of appreciation from the youth minister communicate love and respect for parents of teenagers. Visits in the home, before church services, over a meal, or during a coffee break can build a deeper level of trust and understanding between parents and the youth minister.

Developing a Ministry to Parents

Many youth ministers are beginning to see the benefit of working with parents of youth. These adults influence the lives of youth in significant ways, more than a youth minister could ever hope to do alone. Richard Ross says, "Sometimes you do more for youth by working through adults than you could by working with youth directly."[15]

An adequate philosophy of ministry with parents begins with the question, "Why are we doing this?" Is it because the church across town has a parent ministry, and we must keep up with them? Is it because the parents are looking for some social activities? Or, is it because there is a legitimate need for ministry? In the final analysis, a parent ministry should grow out of a sense of God's guidance and direction for ministry.

Three guidelines for parent ministry will keep the effort going in the right direction. First, work within the church program organizations. Coordinate with others who have responsibility for planning for adults in the church. Do not try to form a maverick group outside the church parameters. Second, allow families to spend time together. Do not overprogram for youth. Every school holiday does not demand another youth activity. Plan time for families to be together. Third, plan parent-youth activities along with activities specifically for youth and parents of youth.

The following are some specific suggestions for ministry with parents:

Parent Council

Invite several parents to build a parent council to plan and conduct the parent ministry. This council should represent the makeup of the group, with single parents, remarried parents, as well as traditional families represented. This group can provide input, guidance, and planning for parent ministry events.

Parent Discussion Groups

Parents of teenagers appreciate the opportunity to meet with other parents and discuss items of interests related to their parenting roles. Parent roundtables, panel discussions, talk-back sessions with the youth minister, and parent fellowships are good times for interchange and fellowship. These times also give the youth minister valuable insight into needs for ministry within the homes of teenagers in the group.

Parent Newsletter

A newsletter specifically for parents is helpful in sharing information and addressing problems facing parents of youth. News of youth events and parent activities can be channeled through a newsletter. A personal note from the youth minister can help develop relationships with parents.

Parent-Youth Events

Events planned for youth and their parents can bridge the communication gap that exists in many families. The chance to laugh together and address some mutual concerns is an important element in parent-youth events. Fellowships, retreats, discussion times, and seminars can be planned for parents and youth together.

Parent-Youth Bible Study and Worship Resources

Provide help for families to develop quality times of Bible study and worship. Many families want to have family devotionals but do not know how to start. Suggest printed resources and offer training times to help families start in family Bible study or worship.

Parent Ministry Meetings

Plan special meetings, luncheons, classes, or seminars for parents of youth. Invite special speakers, schedule a film or video, or offer a forum to address topics of interest to parents of teenagers. These events should always be coordinated with others in the church who have responsibility for adult programming.

The Youth Minister's Relationship with Parents

Youth ministers can be tremendous assets to parents and teenagers. They can support the home and provide the necessary ingredients for a well-rounded ministry with youth in several ways.

First, the church can provide group activities and learning experiences that are beyond the capabilities of the home. Youth are energized and influenced by their peers. A church youth group can be a catalyst for spiritual growth. The positive influence of other Christian teenagers is a powerful force for nurture in a young person's life.

Second, adults who work with youth can be the "significant others" in a teenager's life. These youth leaders can support and reinforce the teachers of Christian parents. I often thank God for the leaders of my own two teenagers. Those leaders have taught my children through words and actions many things our family could not do alone.

Youth leaders can also provide ministry to parents and youth during times of crisis. The home needs youth ministry when the phone rings in the middle of the night and the parent says, "My son has overdosed on drugs and I don't know what to do." The home needs youth ministry when the teenage daughter has just lost her mother to cancer. The home needs youth ministry when the bridges of communication between parent and youth have been burned by harsh words and rebellious actions.

A fourth way youth ministers can help the home is by providing consultation and guidance for parents and youth. Younger youth ministers may feel awkward telling middle-age parents how to rear their children. Playing the role as expert in child-rearing is not the best stance for youth ministers. A better approach is to offer reading materials, resources, magazines, and guest speakers who can offer help to parents and teens. Parent discussion groups can provide opportunities to exchange ideas and gain new insights into parenting roles. Youth ministers with appropriate training can provide pastoral counseling for parents and teenagers.

These ideas work well for those parents who are involved or supportive of the church's youth ministry. However, many teenagers have parents who are non-Christians or not involved with the ministry of the church. Those parents present a challenge to youth ministers who desire a better relationship between home and church. Some cautions will smooth the road toward better relationships.

Youth ministers should resist the temptation to become the "missing parent" for a youth whose parents do not attend church. Many youth will need the encouragement that is missing from their noninvolved parents. Other youth will be from single-parent homes and will not have a meaningful relationship with both parents. A youth minister can be a significant adult and friend to youth, but never a replacement for a parent.

Youth ministers have a responsibility to minister to youth in all facets of their lives. This means we must build bridges between church and home. Parents who are uninvolved with the church may fill neglected and ignored if no efforts are made to reach out to them. Jealousy and doubt may lead them to use the church as a punishment. For example, when the teenager breaks a rule, he is grounded from attending youth group activities.

The home and the church can be a powerful partnership, if there is cooperation from both sides. When there is little evidence of support from parents, the temptation is for the youth minister to become all things to the youth. Parents who are frustrated in the relationships with their teenagers often will turn them over to the church to keep them occupied. Youth ministers should resist the urge to replace the lack of attention from parents in the lives of teenagers in the youth group. There is a need for both kinds of relationships in the lives of youth.

26

Parent-Teen Relationships

Contemporary Parents

As adults reach the middle years, they make a major turn in life. As their teenagers march into a youth culture full of energy, hope, and dreams for the future, middle-age parents let go of their younger years and face the realities of mid-life. This phase of life has some emotional and behavioral dimensions that impact the relationships between teenagers and their parents. It is full of implications for a church's youth ministry.

Parents of teenagers face challenges to their ego, physical resources, emotions, sexuality, vocation, and parenting needs. At the same time, their sons and daughters face similar changes at a different level. This parallel is what Barbara Smith calls the collision between adolescence and "middlescence."[6] The tensions many families face stem from both generations—parents and teens—struggling with similar problems and not understanding how to handle the situation. The following are some of the problems that surface during these years.

Ego Problems

Both teenagers and parents face challenges to their sense of identity. As teenagers sort through images and signals about their identity, their parents struggle with thoughts of lost youth and the reality of aging. Reaching thirty, forty, or fifty years of age can be an emotional time bomb for many middle-age adults. As adolescents race into young adulthood, eyes filled with visions of new frontiers, the middle-age parent is nagged by a life half finished and many dreams left unfulfilled.

Andrea, a ninth-grade girl, confided that she is embarrassed by her mother's behavior. Her thirty-eight-year-old mother started wearing a blond wig, mini-skirts, and attending rock concerts with her. Andrea, who is concerned about her own appearance and acceptance from friends, is now concerned about a mother who is trying to hold onto her fading youthfulness.

Unresolved problems from their own adolescence can create friction between parents and their teenagers. Parents can recall their teenage years and see their sons and daughters facing temptations and problems they faced. Guilt or doubt about past experiences can haunt parents and create confusion in the parenting process.

Body Changes

Changes in the body can require adjustments for teenagers and parents alike. While teenagers are experiencing rapid physical growth and new feelings of strength and physical ability, their parents are feeling a sense of decline in physical strength. Decreased physical stamina, increased physical problems, and a growing awareness of physical limitations are reminders that youthfulness is passing and life is not limitless.

Professional athletes can be "over the hill" at thirty-five. Parents can be caught up in proving they are not yet "over the hill" by frantic attempts at physical exercise, changing to a youthful wardrobe, and competing with their teenagers. This adjustment to physical change at mid-life can cause some parents to have difficulties relating to the needs of their own teenagers.

Emotional Challenges

As parents move into mid-life, they step onto center stage of society. They often feel major responsibilities for the demands of society, church, home, and career. Middle-age adults often feel the need to take stock of life and reevaluate their priorities. They may see for the first time that dreams will not be realized, goals that will not be reached, and advancements will pass on to others.

Death or retirement of friends and loved ones heightens the sense of aging. When the parents of teenagers see their own parents die, grief and depression can bring more than hurt over the loss of a loved one. This experience can be a reminder that death is an inevitable reality and life is short.

Parents struggling with emotional burdens may have little energy to assist their teenagers in emotional stress. A broken date can be traumatic to a teenager. The middle-age parent may have little sympathy for what seems only a minor problem when compared to the problems of mid-life. Teenagers may reasonably grumble, "You just don't understand."

Sexuality

Middle-age adults begin seeing sex in shades of gray about the time their teenagers discover sex in technicolor. The stress of societal demands, menopause, and periods of psychological impotence diminish the luster of youthful sexuality. Middle-age parents begin trying to focus more on socializing than on sexualizing in their relationships. They may subtly envy their teenagers who are emerging as sexual beings. Some parents even resort to asserting their physical vigor by immoral sexual behavior in order to boost their self-esteem or self-confidence.

Vocational Choices

Another challenge facing both teenagers and parents is the way they approach vocational choices. Teenagers face an array of choices. The whole world seems open, beckoning for their energies and talents. At the same time, vocational choices for the parents are closing rapidly.

Many mid-life parents, especially fathers, are haunted by unfulfilled goals and dreams, poor decisions, and work left undone. Interestingly, mothers in mid-life may have greater vocational choices than their husbands. With the passing of the demands of child care, many women launch into new careers at mid-life. This increases the pressure on men who define their self-esteem by their vocational success, as they see career choices closing for them and opening up for their children and spouses.

Parenting

As adolescents move into adulthood, parents may have difficulty in letting go. Separation can be painful for both parents and teenagers, even though adolescents desire freedom to make their own choices. Fear of failure causes some parents to cling too tightly to their teenage children. Some fathers, feeling they have neglected the family in pursuit of career, turn back to the family just as their teenage children want more independence.

The "empty nest" causes parents to take a new look at their roles and brings a reevaluation of the marriage. More responsibility falls on the parents to meet emotional needs of their spouse. Where much attention has been given to the children, the marriage partners may discover they have little in common except parenting.

These challenges present a wealth of opportunities for ministry. Churches can explore ways to assist parents in their emotional, physical, and spiritual needs as well as the relationships with their teenage children. Youth ministry can be expanded to include seminars, discussion groups, retreats, printed materials, sermons, and conferences designed to enrich the lives of middle-age parents. Parent-youth events, such as retreats, fellowships, classes, and discussion groups, could help both teenagers and parents face the common issues of growing up and growing older.

Parents of teenagers are crying out for ministry. Youth ministers stand in the unique position to help "restore the hearts of the fathers to their children, and the hearts of the children to their fathers" (Mal. 4:6).

Parent and Teenager Communication

The Search Institute study found a desire among parents and young adolescents for more communication. "We find that young people want to talk to their parents about issues that interest them, puzzle them, trouble them and that parents want to talk with their children. But, in most instances, the conversations never happen."[7]

In my ministry experiences I have discovered a deep longing on the part of both parents and teenagers for more communication. Parents are frustrated and disturbed when their teenagers do not talk with them. In most cases this is a normal part of the developmental process. Parents often are surprised and confused when their teenager goes through the "cave era"—when she goes into the "cave" and only comes out for food or money. Strangely, teenagers also want more conversation with parents, but they want someone to listen as well as lecture.

Parenting Styles with Teenagers

The young couple near us in the restaurant had several children seated around the table. One of the boys, about age seven, was acting unruly. He stood up and walked around the restaurant, bothered other customers, and nearly tripped one of the waiters. His father took him by the arm and headed for the rest room. When they returned, tears glistened in the eyes of the boy as he carefully sat down in his chair.

Parents of teenagers often wish the conflicts they had with their children could be handled as swiftly and surely as a quick trip to the rest room for a spanking. In the face of accelerating change in today's world, parents may feel inadequate and unprepared to be the parent of an adolescent. Thinking that teenagers do not want interaction with their parents compounds the situation and adds to the confusion.

Parenting teenagers is not a precise science. The proliferation of books, magazine articles, and television shows offering advice on child rearing can help young parents. However, the mass of information can be confusing and tends to imply that expert advice is essential to the task.

Several patterns of parenting emerge in the course of family life. In many cases, parents fall into the routine they experienced as a child. This may be healthy in many instances, but it can be negative and painful if the parents grew up in an undesirable home life.

This situation is compounded when the child reaches adolescence. Parenting teenagers bears little resemblance to parenting preschoolers and children. The relationships and interactions of previous years can build a foundation for positive parent-teen relationships during the adolescent years. Or, they can blossom into confrontation, rebellion, power struggles, and broken communication if the foundation of positive relationships is not laid prior to the teenage years.

The following styles of parenting describe the common ways parents and teenagers interact.

The *drill-sergeant* thrives on control and immediate obedience. This parent expects the teenager to know and obey the rules and wait for the parent to make the decisions. The parent makes the decisions and rarely asks the teenager for input. Love is usually expressed in the form of approval when the teenager performs well. Punishment for breaking any rule, no matter how minor, can be swift and harsh. Teenagers in this environment can be terrors when they are away from their parents. These are youth who "sow the wild oats" on youth trips or when they leave home for college.

The *casual observer* is quite different from the *drill sergeant*. This parent hardly takes notice of the teenager. The parent gives the teenager free rein to do as he or she wishes. At the end of the childhood years, the teenager is allowed to make all decisions with little or no input from the parent. In most cases, these are the youth who are confused and disoriented about themselves. They perceive the lack of attention and guidance from the parent as a lack of love. What the parent thinks is freedom looks like lack of love and caring to the adolescent. These are the most perplexed, mixed-up teenagers I have known.

The *helicopter pilot* loves to hover. This parent smothers the teenager with attention and help. Love and nurture are important to this parent. Where the *drill sergeant* controls by power, the *helicopter pilot* controls by love and manipulation. Teenagers from this environment are often compliant but may be manipulative. They can be skilled at covering their tracks with deceitful behaviors.

The *amusement park guide* exists to make the teenage child happy. The *helicopter pilot* has many of the same characteristics but seeks more control. The *amusement park guide* allows the teenager to make all the decisions and stands by to attend to all the needs. This parent seeks to avoid conflict by giving the teenager the freedom to make all decisions with little or no responsibility for the consequences. Teenagers in this setting tend to be spoiled and irresponsible. They do not know how to respond to correction and have a hard time following through with commitments. Although they enjoy the freedom from responsibilities, they seem to have an intangible desire for loving guidance.

The *consultant* is the most positive style in this group. This parent seeks to guide the teenager to make healthy decisions by gradually turning over responsibilities within appropriate boundaries. The goal of this parent is for the adolescent to be equipped to make most decisions by the time of high school graduation. Parents involve teenagers in the process of decision making in this style of parenting. The parent still retains the final approval, but the teenager is encouraged to be an active part of the process.

This parent maintains a degree of control while gradually turning over freedom to the adolescent. There is a high degree of love as the parent evolves from being provider and controller to teacher and friend.

Teenagers in this style of parent-teen relationships may sometimes appear disrespectful to adults who want to dictate rules for every action. Because they have been encouraged by parents to ask questions and discover how decisions were made, their questioning may appear to be a questioning of adult authority. There is a fine line between the "why" of a teenager wanting to learn how to make mature decisions, and the "why do I have to do what you say" of a teenager who is resisting adult authority.

Effects of Parenting Styles

These parenting styles can be summarized according to the degree of control and degree of love.

Parenting Style	Degree of Control	Degree of Love
Drill Sergeant	High	Low
Casual Observer	Low	Low
Helicopter Pilot	High	High
Amusement Park Guide	Low	High
Consultant	Changing High to Low	High

These styles affect the way teenagers approach life and their relationships with others. Negative behaviors can result from a parental style that is either overly strict or permissive.

Adolescents reared in homes with too much control (autocratic or authoritarian parents) are more likely to show the following behaviors: hostility to parents, difficulty relating to people of different ages, anti-social activities (stealing, lying, fighting, vandalism), feelings of rejection from the peer group, rejection of traditional moral standards, and inability to relate well to people.[8]

Adolescents reared in homes with too little control also exhibit un-desirable traits. Teenagers with parents who are too permissive are more like to show the following behaviors: do not go out of the way to help others; less likely to live by moral standards of parents (with respect to stealing, lying, drinking); more likely to be involved in drugs, sex, and alcohol abuse; and more likely to attend sexually explicit movies.

Desirable, positive behaviors are not taught well in permissive homes. Teenagers from these homes are not as likely to be concerned about people in general, relate well to people, or to be religiously or ethically motivated.[9]

Characteristics of Healthy Parent-Youth Relationships

Ross and Rowatt list several characteristics that are common in healthy parent-youth relationships.[10] These characteristics are:

Conflict

Conflict is a normal reaction to the changes going on in family structure as the teenager grows up and moves toward independence. One of the traits of healthy families is the ability to deal with conflict in non-destructive ways.

Communication

Healthy families are able to give and receive messages at a variety of levels. This involves considering the words said, body language, tone of voice, and communication of feelings.

Affirmation

Healthy families know how to give and receive simple, straight, and direct compliments. They also accept responsibilities for their share of the household chores and for caring for one another.

Openness

Healthy families are open and honest with each other and with those outside the family. A level of trust has developed over the years because of this openness.

Limits

Parents and youth need self-discipline. Family rules that apply to each member strengthen the bonds of the family. Parents should be willing to live by mutual rules for the sake of their children. For example, if the adolescent is expected to finish his chores before going out, then Dad should not play golf until he has finished his responsibilities. If the teenager is expected to call if she is going to be late, then parents should also call to let their teenager know they will be late. Although restrictions may vary between parents and teenagers, parents should model how to live within limits.

Change

Healthy parents and teenagers are able to change to meet the new relationships as the teenager grows older. This flexibility does not mean basic values and commitments are sacrificed. Rather, parents and teenagers are willing to learn to negotiate in order to meet each other's needs. The teenage years are least productive if parents are rigid and unyielding in all areas. Parents whose only response is, "Because I said so" find it difficult to adapt to their child's emerging maturity.

Intimacy

Healthy families share ideas, work, play, and problems together. These facets of life change radically during the adolescent years, and both parties have to adjust. As the child moves into adolescence, he may brush aside the hugs and kisses that he once welcomed. Parents must realize that the teenager still needs physical expressions of love, but not as openly as before. Healthy families also share a spiritual foundation of intimacy. Parents who are able to talk about their faith and intimacy with God give a valuable gift to their teenagers.

Trust

Trust takes years to develop but can be destroyed in one moment. Teenagers learn trust by observing trustworthy parents. When trust is broken, by parent or teenager, it is important to begin immediately to build it back with honesty and integrity.

27

The Role of the Home in Spiritual Growth

Three passages of Scripture offer a picture of the responsibilities parents have for the spiritual nurture of their young. Both Old and New Testament words point toward the biblical position on spiritual responsibilities of the home.

Deuteronomy 6:4-7 begins with the *shema*, the most revered passage of Scripture to the ancient Hebrews. "Hear, O Israel! The Lord is our God, the Lord is one!" were the words spoken so often in Hebrew homes that children often knew these words before they knew their own parent's names. It is no coincidence that the imperative in verses 5-7 follows this important passage. The responsibility for teaching this message lies on the shoulders of parents.

Proverbs 22:6 is a passage well known to parents and children. Parents of teenagers must remember that it says, "when he is old," the child will not depart. It does not say that the child will never waver from the teaching of the parents. Many parents have done their best in rearing their child, only to have their adolescent rebel and reject the religious training of the home. In many cases that child will return to the faith when he is older.

Ephesians 6:1-4 is a favorite of parents, especially the first three verses. However, verse 4 says, "Fathers, do not provoke your children to anger; but bring them up in the discipline and instruction of the Lord." Parents have a clear commission to teach their children the things of God.

The Home Is the Cradle of Theology

The Bible speaks clearly about the responsibility of parents for the spiritual nurture of their children. The home is the first and most important source of religious training. The child first learns the meaning of such things as trust, love, honesty, and faithfulness through the relationships with parents. These concepts are later applied to feelings and beliefs associated with God. A child who grows up with abusive

155

parents suffers a tragic loss, because he or she has difficulty seeing God as loving and protective. The early experiences with parents form the basis of the child's theology.

Parents are also the child's first teachers in the mundane things of life as well as religious areas. Many parents have difficulty teaching their children more than the basic information about God. They may tell Bible stories at bedtime or pray at meals, but these practices fade or disappear during the adolescent years.

Many parents balk at the idea that they are disciplers for their children. They may try to have mealtime prayers, but they shudder and roll their eyes at the suggestion of having family devotions, Bible studies, or discussions about God and the Bible. Fathers and mothers turn too quickly to the church for all the discipling of their teenagers.

The fact remains parents are disciplers whether they try or not. Their children learn from observing, listening, and relating to them. Their life-styles, values, reactions, priorities, and religious commitments speak loudly to their teenagers. Parents are teaching their young about God's place in their lives around the clock.

This is one reason youth ministry should be concerned about ministry with parents. If the messages about God and our relationship to Him received at home are not consistent with those taught at church, there is going to be confusion and inconsistency in the life of the teenager. Youth ministers should work to build the spiritual atmosphere of the *home*.

Relationship Between Youth Ministry at Home and Church

If parents have the primary responsibility for the spiritual training of their young, where does that leave the youth minister? How does the church relate to the home in teaching and training? How do the youth minister and youth leaders relate to parents? What about parents who are not Christians?

These are tough questions, and they demand thought and reflection. If a youth minister is going to build a firm, biblical stance to youth ministry, there must be a place for parents in the process. Parents and youth leaders must work together to guide the teenagers toward God.

Parents have the primary responsibility for religious training of their teenagers. The church's youth ministry must acknowledge this and seek ways to support and encourage parents in their responsibility. Youth ministers who imply, "If you will give me your teenagers and stay away, I'll give them their religious training," are neither biblical nor responsible.

The youth ministry of a church can provide facets of religious training and avenues for ministry outside the resources of the home. The youth minister and youth leaders can be significant adults who model a consistent Christian life-style for teenagers. They stand as guarantors of the promises of God for teenagers. They teach biblical truths and show teenagers what an adult Christian looks like. The home needs the fellowship of other Christians to complete the religious training of teenagers.

Both the home and the church perform religious education, but they do it in different ways. The church generally adapts the classroom approach to teaching. There are teachers, lesson plans, teaching methods, and an age-group setting. This may be more informal at times, but the pattern is still the same. The learning session usually proceeds from presentation of content, to a learning goal, and then to suggestions for application in the lives of the learners. Hopefully, the teens will put into practice what they experience in the classroom. The sequence then is *purposeful teaching* leading to *living the example*.

The home is also a teaching institution but not necessarily like the classroom. The lessons are generally lived out in the context of family life-style. Then they are explained and discussed in more or less informal ways. Family traditions and discussions provide the markers that help us understand the lessons we learn through living in the home. The sequence for this type of teaching is *purposeful living* followed by *teaching and discussion*. The application precedes the lesson. The learning experience goes on continually in the home. Children learn from their parents and siblings by observing, hearing, and interacting.

The church teaches a lesson and then suggests ways to apply the lesson. The home lives out the application and then explains what has happened. Both can work together to reinforce and support one another. If either is teaching opposing ideas, the learners—teenagers in this case—are going to be confused or frustrated.

Strommen and Strommen point out that a little over half the young adolescents in the Search Institute study indicated a desire for receiving more help from their parents on what it means to be a Christian. The loving, informal atmosphere of a healthy family provides a wonderful setting for this help. Strommen and Strommen say:

> When young people learn that parents are committed to open discussion carried on in a spirit of humility, they will grow in their ability to share personal experiences and ideas. It is in this kind of atmosphere also that the strength of a parent's faith comes through to a child, as, for instance, in a time of great stress.[11]

28

Reaching the Nonchurch Parents

Is This My Job?

Many youth ministers find growing numbers of youth attending church without their parents. In every youth group, some complain because their parents made them come to church, and a significant number who are there managed to come alone. These youth are growing up without the important link between home and church. They feel left out on parent-youth night. They do not see their parents at the parents' meeting before youth camp. They lack the model of parents being involved in the work of the church.

The youth minister has a real challenge in reaching nonchurch teenagers. Why should we be concerned with reaching out to nonchurch adults? Isn't that someone else's job? How can we spend the time and effort to reach adults when it takes so much energy just planning for youth?

Ministry with youth means being involved in every area of life. When we minister with youth *alone*, we ignore the role of parents in the life of the teenager. We may attempt to bypass the influence of parents on youth, but we cannot ignore this vital relationship.

Jamie was very active in the youth group, but her parents did not attend church. Since she was active, the youth minister felt it was not necessary to visit her parents. Jamie came to all the church services and most youth activities, sang in the youth choir, and even served on the youth ministry council. However, her parents began using the church youth activities as a form of punishment. When Jamie broke any rule, her parents grounded her from attending the next youth group event.

Parents who are not involved in church may look upon the church as a competitor. They sometimes become jealous or envious of the attention their teenager gives to the youth group or the leaders in the group. When conflicts occur between parents and the youth the church may become a weapon of comparison for either group.

This situation could be avoided by good relationships between the youth leaders and parents. Jealousy can be diffused when the parents know the youth minister and reach some level of trust and mutual understanding. The level of trust may not be the same as with parents who are involved in the church, but at least the parents can realize the youth minister is not a threat.

Reaching the Nonchurch Parents

Reaching out to nonchurch parents of youth is not the job for youth ministers alone. It can be done best in coordination with other people in the church. The following are some suggestions for reaching out to parents of youth who do not attend church.

First, share the names of nonchurch parents of youth with adult Sunday School workers. Those people can extend an invitation to the nonchurch adults to become a part of a class or group of their peers in the church. The adult Sunday School classes may not be aware of the connection the family has with the church through the youth ministry. The parents are more likely to come when they are contacted by adults of their own age group.

Second, ask other parents of youth to invite the nonchurch parents to attend functions of the church. This is especially helpful when there are parent-youth activities planned. An invitation from another parent carries a lot of influence.

A third suggestion is to invite the nonchurch parents to a special seminar, fellowship, or activity designed for parents of teenagers. Parents often look for help with their parenting challenges. They may respond to some practical helps to their parental needs offered by the church.

Another suggestion is one I have found to be very helpful with parents who do not attend church. Invite the nonchurch parents to host a youth fellowship in their home. Parents often look for ways to be involved in the lives of their teenagers, but they do not always know how to start. This is a simple way to build better parent-youth relationships and reach out to nonchurch parents. Offer to supply all the food, the program, and even plenty of adult chaperons. The fellowship time between the other youth leaders and the nonchurch parents can be a positive experience.

Parent-youth activities provide a fifth way to reach out. Adults who do not attend church may need an easy way to start coming. It takes some effort the first time to get up Sunday morning, get dressed, drive to the church, find the right class, and meet strangers in the group. A parent-youth event can provide the motivation to make the effort. Their youth, who is already involved, can help the parents find their way around.

Finally, meeting in a neutral location makes it easier for many non-church parents to break the ice and become involved in church. The church building may seem imposing. Many parents' events, seminars, fellowships, and discussions can be scheduled in members' homes. A local restaurant could be reserved for a meal and discussion. Hotel meeting rooms or other public facilities provide neutral sites for youth-parent meetings. As they become accustomed to the group, non-church parents will find it easier to move into the church setting for future events.

29

Single-Parent and Blended Families

The shape of families is changing from traditional patterns to a variety of forms. The statistics tell the story. In 1955, 60 percent of the families in the United States consisted of a working father, a homemaker mother, and two or more children. By 1985, that kind of family unit had dropped to only 7 percent.[12] The United States Bureau of the Census predicts that 59 percent of the children growing through the teenage years during the latter part of the twentieth century will live for a period of time with only one parent. Here is the breakdown:

12 percent born out of wedlock
40 percent born to parents who divorce
5 percent born to parents who separate
2 percent born to parents who die
59 percent living with only one parent

This means that less than half the youth we work with (41 percent) will live in a two-parent family. In 1970, only 10 percent of the families with children were headed by a single parent. From 1970 to 1984 the number of divorced mothers who headed families increased by 300 percent.[13]

These figures cannot be taken lightly if we are to minister effectively with youth and their families. Single-parent homes and blended families made up of remarried adults and children from previous marriages present serious problems that must be considered.

The Problems

Aside from the grief and loss of a ruptured family, what are the problems presented by single-parent or blended families? How do these problems effect youth ministry?

Transportation is a simple but perplexing problem for single-parent families. If the teenager is not able to drive or if there is only one car in the family, the single parent may not be able to transport the teenager to many youth activities. The youth may have to depend on other teenagers or a youth leader for transportation. This is especially troublesome for new people in the group who may not know anyone to call for help.

Strained relationships with a stepparent or step-siblings is a common problem in blended families. When divorced parents of teenagers remarry, they thrust their teenager into a new relationship with a parent figure. Neither the stepparent nor the teenager has the years of love, nurture, bonding, and family experiences to build a new relationship. They each are starting with no foundation at a time when parent-youth relationships are tested in the best of families.

Many teenagers react to divorce of their parents with a mixture of anger, frustration, and grief. They often blame themselves for the breakup of their family. "If only I had been a better kid . . . !" "If only I had not asked for so much money . . . !" "If I had not been on the telephone so much . . . !" They fear betrayal and are anxious about relationships with the opposite sex, marriage, and personal commitments. They alternate between resenting the missing parent and grieving over the loss of that parent's relationship.

Teenagers from divorced families often spend time with the noncustodial parent on a regular basis. Some teenagers live with one parent during the week and visit the other parent during the weekends. Other teenagers live with the other parent during the summer. This creates havoc with participation in youth activities. When the teenager starts dating, he may resent the time spent with the other parent because he is prevented from seeing friends on the weekends.

Single-parent families commonly live on strict budgets. Making ends meet on one income can be difficult. The single parent may have to pay for child care. Youth activities that require a sum of money may prevent youth in single-parent homes from participating. Youth camp, ski trips, choir tours, and uniforms for the youth choir musical may be an economic burden for single-parent families.

Single parents often do not attend parent activities at church. They may be so busy trying to manage the family alone or working at multiple jobs that they are unable to attend meetings. Some single parents fear that the church group will reject them because they are divorced. Unfounded fears and embarrassment keep them from the place that could be a major source of encouragement and support.

When teenagers in single-parent families start to date, they lack the input from two parents. This can be a loss when the youth needs guidance about healthy male-female relationships.

New sibling relationships in blended families present other problems. When a man and woman with teenagers from a previous marriage marry, the teenagers find themselves with new sisters or brothers. This situation opens the door for multiple family problems. What does the teenager do if the new sibling takes over her room or the car? What if the new sibling is so obnoxious and rebellious that peaceful coexistence is impossible? What if he "falls in love" with his new sister?

Finally, discipline problems between the teenager and the stepparent are common. Parents normally struggle with discipline and parent-youth relationships without the added dimension of being a stepparent. Worries about how they are doing bother 66 percent of the mothers and 60 percent of the fathers in the Search Institute study of parents and teenagers.[14] This problem is also compounded for stepparents.

Suggestions for Ministry

These problems need to be addressed. We cannot simply brush aside the situation of single-parent and blended families as another symbol of a corrupt society. There are several ways youth ministry can offer a cup of cool water to those who are hurting in the midst of changes in the family.

First, support groups for youth from single-parent or blended families can offer a place to deal with the issues. These groups could meet after school, following other church activities, or at times and places away from traditional church meetings. These groups should not meet during regularly scheduled church classes, since youth should be involved with their peers at these meetings. The group leader should assume a role as facilitator and encourager for the youth as they discuss their common problems. The message of hope and the promise of new life in Christ can come through in this healing ministry with youth.

Support groups for single-parents or remarried parents with teenagers are a second suggestion for ministry. These groups could be similar to the support groups for youth. The groups could meet at the same time, in a different place from the youth groups. Such a group would offer parents a chance to discuss and evaluate the challenges facing them as they rear their teenagers.

A third suggestion for ministry is to address the issues of single-parenting or stepparenting in seminars and classes at church. Offer a special interest class to help parents deal with the problems facing them in these situations.

Fourth, parent-youth retreats provide the opportunity to enhance mutual relationships. This could be particularly beneficial to busy single-parents or those stepparents looking for ways to build relationships with their teenagers.

Finally, plan all youth and parent events with consideration for transportation and limited finances. Look for ways to make it easier for parents to participate, especially if they are new to the church activities.

Part 5
The Church Staff Youth Minister

30

Calling and Preparation

The Call to Youth Ministry

God directs lives in many ways. For some people the call to ministry is remarkable and clear. For others the call is a subtle encouragement by those who see in them the gifts for ministry.

I felt God's leadership toward a life of ministry when I was a teenager but did not understand the specific area of ministry for several years. It was not until I finished college studies, served in the military, and worked as a high school band director that I sensed the specific direction of God's leadership for my life. After serving two different churches in youth ministry positions, I came to realize the clear need for adequate preparation for youth ministry.

The call to serve God through youth ministry has been a clear, enduring call in my life. The call to youth ministry is a valid, lifelong call to serve God through a ministry with youth, their families, and the adults who lead youth. It is not a stepping-stone to some larger or more important ministry. It is not something to do to gain a little experience until one can move into a "real" ministry position. I have seen this testimony in the lives of countless youth ministers who have served faithfully for years on church staffs, in denominational positions, in writing and consulting ministries, and in individual speaking and teaching endeavors.

Youth ministry, like many other forms of ministry, does not have to be a full-time, paid position to be valid. Many persons are serving as part-time or bivocational youth ministers. Still others are serving voluntarily as the coordinator of a church's youth ministry. These persons may find themselves responsible for the ministry with youth because they are the only ones in the church who work with youth. Still others are called to be full-time vocational youth ministers. These are all legitimate forms of youth ministry.

Preparation for Youth Ministry

The calling to ministry is the first step in preparation for youth ministry. Aside from the profession of faith in Christ, the call to ministry is the most important element in the Christian worker's pilgrimage. A sense of divine leadership pointing toward a lifetime of service to God is necessary for effective ministry with youth.

A sincere love for and sympathetic understanding of youth is a second step toward preparation for youth ministry. Youth ministry can evolve into a series of rote activities and meaningless tasks without a desire to touch the lives of youth in all the spheres of life.

The calling to a life of ministry joins with the sincere love for youth in a desire to serve God through the specific ministry with youth. This is the third step toward preparation for a youth ministry. Those who want to serve as youth ministers should feel a call to that ministry rather than looking at youth ministry as a way of paying their dues before moving on to some other form of Christian vocation.

A fourth step toward preparation for youth ministry is experience as a volunteer youth leader. A young man once asked me about the possibility of assuming a youth ministry position in a rather large church. I asked if he had worked with youth in the church where he was a member. Although there was a need for several volunteer youth leaders in his church, he had never desired to work with youth as a volunteer leader. I advised him to take one of the volunteer positions, gain some experience in youth leadership, and then decide if that was the area of ministry God had in mind for him.

Training in workshops, seminars, and conferences affords youth leaders a level of preparation that was not available even a few years ago. A fifth step of preparation is to attend as many of these training experiences as possible. They will put you in touch with the latest knowledge, skills, and materials for working with youth. They will also help build relationships with the community of those with common interests in youth ministry.

A sixth step is available for college students who desire study in youth ministry. Some colleges and universities offer basic courses in adolescent development and church youth ministry. College students should not specialize too quickly in one particular area of ministry. College study is the time for broad-based liberal arts education. Although some specific courses in youth ministry are available, in-depth training in this area should be focused on the seminary level.

Seminary education is a seventh step for studying youth ministry.

Seminary provides the theological and practical base for Christian vocation and long-term ministry. Although some churches call youth ministers who have no college or seminary background, the most effective youth ministry grows out of appropriate training.

Some Suggested Courses of Study

College/University Level

A broad liberal arts education is the preferred route for preparation for ministry. A major in religion or Bible is one option, but not the only possible major. Courses in religion, religious education, and Bible are helpful as preparation for seminary. Studies in English, math, psychology, sciences, and history are important. Some courses in foreign languages may be helpful in dealing with the languages on the seminary level.

Seminary Level

A solid foundation is necessary in the following areas: Bible, theology, evangelism, Christian history, church administration, philosophy of education, educational psychology, principles of teaching, child and adolescent development, adult development, recreation, communication, and youth ministry courses. Some field experience in a youth ministry position is also essential.

I often have students in seminary classes who have had youth ministry courses on the college level. Some have asked, "What is left to learn about youth ministry? I know how to plan a youth calendar, lead youth Bible studies, and lead youth activities. I even know how to counsel with youth and have performed discipleship with youth. What else is there to learn?" I have seen those same students amazed at the levels of knowledge and training opened before them in seminary classes. Youth ministry on the seminary level is much more than learning a few rudimentary techniques of youth group leadership.

College is a time for building foundations of knowledge and skills. It is a time for gaining a broad-based education in the common essentials of human knowledge. Introductory courses in religion, religious education, Bible, and youth ministry are appropriate.

Seminary is a time for building the theological and practical underpinnings for ministry. Specialized courses of study, especially in youth ministry, equip the student with skills for effective youth ministry. In the seminary where I serve, the preferred course of study for youth ministers is the Master of Arts in Religious Education with a concentration in Youth Education.

31

Personal Spiritual Growth

My first full-time youth ministry experience is etched in my memory for several reasons. The church was warm and supportive. The youth and leaders were involved, energetic, and filled with hope. The staff members were dedicated Christians who gave their best. However, I ran dry of spiritual reserves within the first year of church service.

During the busy activities of leading youth ministry, directing the youth choir, and filling in for the minister of music who had moved to another church, I forgot to attend to my own spiritual needs. I substituted planning youth Bible study sessions for my own personal devotional Bible reading. I spoke with God only in public prayers, forgetting to converse with Him in private. Sharing my testimony and witnessing became routine duties to be performed.

I faced this dilemma during a retreat for youth ministers sponsored by our state convention. As I traveled alone across the state to the weekend retreat, I realized the extent of my yearning for a closer relationship with Jesus Christ. The sessions at the retreat seemed to be aimed directly at my need to stop relying on my own personal resources and to start drawing from the endless supply of strength and wisdom available from God. The long drive home was a continuous prayer of confession and commitment to God.

The Work of Youth Ministry and Spiritual Growth

I learned several lessons about spiritual needs from that experience. First, it is easy to neglect personal spiritual growth in the midst of planning for youth ministry. Planning for the needs of others is not the same as planning for your own spiritual needs.

Second, planning to teach youth Bible studies is not the same as reading and studying God's Word for your own needs. Some of the hardest times my students face occur when they study for their Bible courses but neglect personal devotional Bible reading. Studying to take a test or preparing to teach a Bible lesson is not the same as reading the Bible for a word of wisdom or instruction from God.

A third lesson I learned about personal spiritual growth is that private worship cannot be replaced by a busy work schedule. This may seem obvious, but much of the work of youth ministry appears to be so spiritual that there seems to be no need for additional moments of worship. Visiting people in the hospital, counseling with teenagers and their families, telling people about Christ, and leading public worship would appear to be enough to fill any need for private times alone with God. These actions, no matter how holy and blessed, do not suffice for the quiet moments of worship and reflection with the Master.

Finally, prayer should saturate every aspect one's of life. God desires the communion of Christians through prayer. Through words and thoughts we converse with the One who loves and desires the special times of reflection and communication with us. Through prayer we gain insights into ministry, strength to face the events of life, guidance through the haze of confusion, and answers to life's problems.

Elements of Spiritual Growth

Time Alone with God

Some time should be spent alone in quiet praise and reflection with God on a regular basis. No matter how busy the daily schedule may be, there is no substitute for at least a few minutes of meditation and prayer. This will prepare your heart and mind for the day's events, or it can draw the strings of closure at the end of the day.

Devotional Bible Reading

The Bible is a treasure of wisdom suitable for study throughout a lifetime. One of the best ways to approach this storehouse of truth is through devotional reading. Many times a passage of Scripture that I have studied for a previous lesson will leap from the pages with new meaning for my life. As I read the words for pleasure of discovering God's message for my life, I can sense new energy to serve Him daily.

Regular Bible Study

Along with devotional Bible reading, a personal plan of Bible study is an important element of spiritual growth. This is a time to dig into the Scriptures in a disciplined, purposeful investigation and study. Several approaches to Bible study can be used. Word, book,exegetical, topical, and character studies have all proven helpful. Set aside a block of time weekly for your own personal plan of Bible study.

Sharing Faith in Witness and Testimony

I know of nothing that is a greater motivator for personal spiritual growth than regularly sharing your faith with non-Christians. We can read and study volumes about the Bible, learn all the facts in the Bible, and memorize endless verses from the Bible and still never tell anyone about the good news of Jesus Christ. I have found that it is nearly impossible to share my faith with non-Christians without being driven back to God's Word for instruction, nourishment, and inspiration. It is too easy to be surrounded by Christians at church and insulated from the world of people who do know Christ. Full-time vocational youth ministers must strive to discover and build relationships with non-Christians in order to share faith through witness and testimony.

Stewardship of Finances

God blesses in material ways by providing for our physical needs. The Bible teaches the principles of stewardship, which includes returning a portion of our income as worship and praise to God. An important element in personal spiritual growth involves offering the tithe and other gifts back to God.

Fellowship and Worship with Believers

As we minister with other Christians, we come together for worship and praise. Even though this is an act of public worship, it has important implications for personal spiritual growth. Corporate worship and informal fellowship serves to nurture the body of Christ because of the nature of Christian life. The spiritual gifts of Christians build up the body by encouraging individuals in the body of Christ. Handshakes, smiles, hugs, an arm around the shoulder during difficult times, a word of encouragement, prayer, praise, and proclamation are just a few of the benefits of fellowship and worship with believers.

Ministry to Hurting People

God blesses the service of His people through the sense of joy that comes in ministry to others. Jesus exhibited the model of servanthood throughout His earthly ministry. Personal spiritual growth can come from following that model of caring for the needs of others.

Reading Devotional Books

Many good devotional books are available today. These can be helpful as inspirational reading for the youth minister. Biographies, daily devotional materials, Christian classics, family devotional resources, and general devotional books have all been helpful sources for personal spiritual growth.

A Network of Support

Personal growth also comes from the relationships with other people. Friends inside and outside the church family can be a source of strength and growth. It is difficult to be an effective leader without a network of support. Friends who offer encouragement, insight, and feedback can be valuable sources of support.

Gary and Jean were friends in a church where I served as a youth minister. Our families loved to head for the woods and spend time roughing it in tents. The cool evenings we spent around the campfire warmed our hearts and nurtured our souls as only friends can do.

Friends outside the church family can also be in the network of support. Bob and Jane were two such friends. We first developed our friendships in the same church. When we moved away, we still maintained the friendship with them through telephone calls and letters. Through the years we remained in contact and planned ways to be together on special occasions. Their friendship has been a source of fond memories and valuable support.

Look for ways to develop friendships among church members and those outside the immediate church family. Develop a network of friends who can provide help to see your strengths as well as your flaws. Honest, loving communication between friends is a gift from God that enhances personal spiritual growth.

Personal Habits and Spiritual Growth

Hobbies are important ways to enhance life and rejuvenate the routines we fall into. A hobby that takes the mind off worries can be a source of relaxation and new energy.

Good health habits may seem mundane, but they can also be important ways to remain spiritually healthy. We don't like to talk about the sin of gluttony, but overeating can be a barrier to spiritual growth. Good disciplines in eating and care for your body spill over into good disciplines in the spiritual realm.

Physical exercise is another dimension of personal spiritual growth. Set aside a time for regular physical exercise, and it will help the mental, emotional, and spiritual components of life as well.

Workaholism is an ailment of modern times. We may find ourselves hemmed in by busy schedules and pressing demands of contemporary society. Personal spiritual growth demands that we find time for relaxation and refreshment in the midst of the race of life. Time spent with family or in personal relaxation will reap a valuable harvest. Jesus often pulled aside for retreats and times of rest. The stress of modern ministry requires that we do the same.

32

Balancing Work and Family

One of the perennial concerns of youth ministers is how to balance the demands of modern youth ministry with a good family life. How does one spend appropriate amounts of time with youth, parents of youth, youth leaders, and other church staff members and still find time and energy to devote to spouse and children? This question also faces single youth ministers who must carve out some time for personal interests apart from the tasks of youth ministry.

Each year we offer a youth ministry lab at the seminary where I teach. Youth ministers and spouses come from all over the United States for a weekend of fellowship, relaxation, and training. We usually offer at least one class dealing with the issue of balancing family needs with youth ministry demands. This class is almost always packed to capacity!

Spouse or Assistant Youth Minister?

The bright, attractive couple sat across from my desk. They shared the news of an interview with a church that was considering the man for a youth ministry position. Both were excited and filled with hope for the future.

"It's such a good church! And the people seem so friendly and eager to have us come to work there. We think this may be where God wants us to serve," the young man said enthusiastically. His wife was smiling and nodding in agreement.

"What do you think about the situation?" I asked the wife.

"Oh, it looks great. I just want to go on all the retreats, teach in Sunday School, and really get to know the youth," she said. She was obviously ready to get involved.

The future looked promising and full of joy for this young couple, but there was a cloud hanging over them that often plagues young couples eager to start in youth ministry. When the man who is a youth minister considers his wife as an assistant youth minister, the cloud can develop into a storm of stress, hurt feelings, and depression.

Married men sometimes give the impression that their wives are there to assist them in every detail of youth ministry. The church receives two youth ministers for the price of one. The wife soon begins to feel used and taken for granted. The teaching position that nobody wants becomes hers. When there are too few sponsors for the youth trips, she is volunteered to go. She is cornered by irate church members who want to complain because the youth behaved poorly during the worship service. Soon she loses her identity and simply becomes an extension of her husband's job.

There is a fine line between teamwork and taking a spouse for granted. The spouse of a youth minister, male or female, can be a tremendous source of encouragement and support. However, the level of involvement should be the choice of the spouse. The spouse should be able to choose whether or not to go on the next youth retreat or accept the teaching position in the youth division. The spouse should feel free to decide whether to be involved in the youth division or another area of the church's ministry.

Many effective youth ministers are married to someone who feels more comfortable in working with children, adults, or the music ministry of the church. When both marriage partners are highly involved in youth ministry, the pressures of time and interpersonal relationships usually follow them home from the office. No one is there to share problems and stresses because both partners are burdened with the same concerns. As children grow older, the problems of time and attention seem to multiply when both marriage partners are always busy with the youth at church.

Most of these problems can be handled during the initial interviews with the search committee or pastor. The question of involvement of the spouse should be discussed openly and freely. Expectations of the church and desires of the potential staff member should be clearly explained to avoid future conflicts on the level of involvement of the spouse.

Spend Time with the Family

An exciting youth ministry calls for many hours at night, on weekends, and during holidays. Nights away from home or family can create problems. Most of these problems can be avoided by observing some simple guidelines.

First, reserve at least one night a week for free time. Although this seems like too little, I am always amazed to find youth ministers who do not spend even this amount of time at home. They feel they must always be spending time with the youth in order to be effective. Or, they feel like the church expects them to be busy with the youth every evening. A free night will be respected and honored by church members if they understand your motives.

Second, spend time with your spouse. The marriage partner is the greatest source of encouragement and joy in a healthy relationship. The marriage relationship can suffer when it is neglected and ignored. I have a friend who presents a single rose to his wife every Friday. It takes a little effort and planning, but his wife looks forward to this sign of affection every week. Even though this youth minister works in a very busy, metropolitan church, he finds time to spend with his wife every week.

Another guideline to help with family relationships is to put your activities on the calendar. Put family birthdays, your wedding anniversary, vacations, and holidays on the calendar. Do not plan a major event at the same time as an important family function. The play at school or the baseball game may seem insignificant, but it may be a big event in your child's eyes. How can we justify spending all our time helping other people's teenagers, when we ignore our own children? When our activities are on the calendar, it is much easier to say, "I'm sorry. That date is already filled." Most people will understand and try to work around conflicts in calendar planning.

Sharpen Skills in Ministry

In my research with older youth ministers, several suggestions were given that have proven helpful in balancing youth and family needs. These often involved sharpening the skills of ministry and developing administrative techniques in order to carve out more quality time to be with family.

Develop the Art of Delegation

Younger youth ministers seem to have the most difficulty with this ministry skill. Their fear is that delegation will appear to be a way for the youth minister to get out of work. Others hesitate to delegate because they have been turned down or let down in the past and it is easier to do the job themselves. As the jobs become more complex and numerous, more and more time is demanded of the youth minister.

Delegation is a compliment to many people. Rather than feeling insulted, most people sense trust and respect when they are asked to assume a responsibility. Delegation is not a way to get out of work. Rather, it is a wise way to multiply the energies of many people and do a better job of ministry.

Emphasize Evangelism and Discipleship

Youth ministry falls short when it becomes simply a Christian social club. The wild and crazy events of youth ministry that entertain and appeal to youth are appropriate when they fit into the larger purpose of fulfilling the Great Commission.

Youth ministry that is built solidly on Bible study and discipleship, that reaches out in evangelism to persons near and far and that is saturated with Christian love and nurture will prove stable and long lasting. The social activities that demand so much time will not have to be promoted because they are competing with other attractions of the world. Instead, fellowship will grow out of Christian *koinonia* because the body of Christ is vibrant and energized with inner strength.

Plan Quality Events, Not Just Quantity Events

The first clue that told me we were living in an overscheduled society was when I noticed younger adolescents pulling out pocket calendars to check their appointments. As we planned a fellowship for our eighth grade group, we had difficulty finding a Saturday that was free for an activity.

The calendar may look empty, but in reality there are few open dates in the schedules of most teenagers. School activities, jobs, sports activities, special classes, and family plans cry out for time. When we plan a youth activity, we are usually presenting another choice among several choices for a teenager's time.

This calls for quality rather than quantity programming. An empty date on the calendar does not require another youth activity. Every school holiday does not have to be filled with a youth group trip or retreat. Quality programming means we plan youth events and activities according to the needs of the group rather than because there is a free date on the calendar.

Quality programming will result in more time for attending to other needs in the youth minister's life. Quality programming also requires that we give our best in planning so that youth will benefit the most by participating in the event. The next time there is a choice between the church youth activities and some other attraction, the quality of the church youth ministry will be remembered.

Equip Volunteers to Lead Activities

I learned this lesson when I was responsible for four different youth softball teams in our church softball league. The teams played every Saturday in different parts of the city. I also had a son who was playing on a baseball team that played games on Saturday every week. I could not attend all four of the youth games and the games of my son. I was forced to do something that turned into a valuable asset to our youth ministry.

I enlisted four coaches and equipped them to be responsible for the youth softball teams. They each enlisted assistant coaches and became capable leaders in our youth ministry. I watched as those coaches provided athletic and spiritual leadership for our youth. It became a joy for me to attend the games, fellowship personally with the youth and parents at the games, and still have time for my own son's baseball games. There were times when I did not attend every game our youth softball teams played, but I knew they were in good hands. Our youth ministry was multiplied because volunteer leaders were equipped to lead youth activities.

Some Sticky Problems

Two problems arise that relate to a youth minister's family and their involvement in youth ministry. One problem involves the spouse and the other revolves around younger children.

We have already discussed the role of the youth minister's spouse in youth ministry. Some insensitive members may expect the spouse to attend every youth event or know every detail of the youth ministry. How do we respond when someone implies that the spouse should be present for all youth events?

There is no easy solution to this problem, but it can often be handled with a gentle reminder that the spouse has other responsibilities and is not expected to be a counselor for every youth activity. Participation and involvement in youth ministry should grow out of a love and desire for ministry with youth instead of pressures from others to participate.

The second problem revolves around how younger children of the youth minister should participate in youth events. Generally, younger children should be left at home with a sitter. On a few occasions, younger children can accompany their parent, but this should be the exception rather than the rule.

I have known several youth ministers who followed this practice and reaped rewards when their children entered the teenage years. The children had not attended youth events as a young child, so they looked forward to being in the youth group. This decision meant that the spouse of the youth minister often stayed at home with children when youth activities were planned. Both children and parents benefited from this approach.

When young children attend youth events, they demand a lot of attention. The youth may enjoy their presence, or they may grow to resent the children being around. The children may not understand why they do not have the attention of their parent. One parent is usually stretched in two directions—trying to tend to a younger child and trying to be a youth leader at the same time.

Although there may be times when younger children can attend some youth activities, a general rule should be to reserve this for their own teenage years. Parents and children will both benefit.

33

Growing Older in Youth Ministry

A few years ago many youth ministers felt their years of service were limited by age. Whenever a youth minister reached the age considered "old," they moved out of youth ministry into some other area of ministry. Some even left the ministry in search of a vocation that was not limited by age.

Churches contributed to this dilemma by calling only younger adults to lead their youth ministry. Stereotypes of youthful, athletic, photogenic heroes were fixed in the minds of search committees as they interviewed prospective youth ministers. However, the realities of the challenges facing today's leaders in youth ministry have caused churches and youth ministers to take a new look at the value of wisdom and experience that comes with maturity.

Research with Older Youth Ministers

Contact over the years with youth ministers over thirty, forty, and fifty years of age prompted me to do some research in this area. I have often supported the concept of staying in youth ministry beyond age thirty, or whatever age youth ministers are considered "old." My experience has reinforced that idea as I have served as a youth minister, youth professional, and now a volunteer youth leader into the middle adult years.

I surveyed a group of older youth ministers (those in the mid-thirties and older) to seek their responses to several questions about youth ministry. By asking for names of other youth ministers in this age group, a list of forty-one names was compiled. Questionnaires were sent to them and over 90 percent completed and returned the forms. This high rate of response indicates a serious interest in this subject.

The average age of the sample was 39.5 years. Ages ranged from 32 to 55. The youth ministers had been serving at their present church for an average of 6.6 years. They had been at their previous church for an average of 4.3 years. The group of youth ministers had been serving for an average of 18.2 years in youth ministry.

Older youth ministers do not necessarily serve in larger churches.

180

The youth ministers interviewed reported their total church membership ranging from 477 to 19,890. Total youth Sunday School enrollment ranged from 45 to 1,298. Average attendance for youth Sunday School ranged from 29 to 600 in the group.

Changing Relationships

Older youth ministers were asked about their relationships with the groups involved in youth ministry. They were asked to describe ways in which their relationships with youth, youth leaders, parents of youth, and fellows staff members had changed. The responses were encouraging and enlightening.

Relationships with the youth were changed, mostly for the better. Rather than becoming weaker as the youth minister grows older, personal relationships become stronger and deeper. The youth feel freer to come to the youth minister with their problems. As one youth minister puts it, "Youth come more readily now with deeper problems. . . . Youth come to me now with purpose, not as much to just hang around." There seems to be a growing respect from the youth as the youth minister gains maturity.

Most of the youth ministers reported that they spend less time with the youth personally, but the time they spend with youth is rewarding and beneficial. Most feel they spend an appropriate amount of time with youth. They spend more time with adults than in earlier years. They see themselves as less "buddy-buddy" with the youth and more like a father/mother figure. "Although I feel that I am just as effective in working with youth, I do feel that they see me differently, more like a father or role model than a close friend," writes one youth minister. Some of the youth ministers have younger interns or assistants who spend large amounts of time with the youth. Others enlist younger volunteer leaders who fulfill the time demands of "hanging out" with youth.

Older youth ministers feel less threatened by teenage rejection or acceptance. "Because of the maturing of my own self-concept, I feel less of the need to be 'popular' with youth," reports a youth minister. Many of the older youth ministers reported that during earlier years they were more concerned about being liked by the youth. They put a lot of effort into winning friendship. Now they worry less about that and feel comfortable in being themselves. The result is an authenticity and integrity that youth sense and respect. The youth recognize the older youth ministers as adults who love and care for them without the artificial trappings of an overgrown adolescent.

Volunteer youth leaders receive more time, attention, and focus with older youth ministers. One youth minister states, "The older I am, the better I am able to relate to leaders and lead, train, motivate, and minister to them." They have a growing respect for the youth leaders and the valuable contributions they make to the youth ministry.

As the youth minister and the volunteer leaders grow closer in age, the youth minister also senses a closeness in personal relationships. They sense more respect from the youth leaders and develop more confidence in leading the volunteers in ministry. The youth minister and leaders see themselves in a peer relationship. "The leaders are peers and experience me in that adult-to-adult or parent-to-parent role," writes a forty-eight year old youth minister. This tends to build support and encouragement for mutual efforts in youth ministry.

Confidence also lends itself to a sense of teamwork in ministry. The older youth minister sees the volunteers as partners in ministry rather than helpers for activities. This encourages the youth minister in planning for more training and team building efforts in the future.

Relationships have changed in similar ways between the older youth ministers and parents of youth. As the youth ministers moved into middle adulthood, they are accepted as peers by the parents of the teenagers. This contributes to a growing respect and feelings of teamwork and trust on the part of parents. A forty-two-year-old youth minister reports, "Many parents are my best friends. I work more with parents now and am not as much considered a threat to family life."

Many of the youth ministers have children who are teenagers or older elementary age. The parents of youth realize the mutual understanding of the challenges of parenting teenagers respond by coming to the youth minister with problems and concerns of family life. "Since I have teens I'm called on more for counseling," states a youth minister. The older youth minister is seen as a trusted adviser and counselor by the parents as well as by the youth.

Most of the older youth ministers reported renewed interests in programming for parents along with activities only for youth. Recognized needs for ministry with parents results in fellowships, seminars, discussions, retreats, and opportunities for input from the parents. Parent and youth activities and activities involving parents, youth, and youth leaders are also planned. This builds a richness and diversity to youth ministry that has often been neglected in the past.

Relationships with the pastor and other church members seems to change as the youth minister grows older. Most report a growing respect from the pastor, although some still hear questions like, "What will you do when you grow up?" While younger youth ministers may function as an important part of a church staff, older youth ministers are often treated with more respect and esteem. Their ideas are sought and valued. A typical response was, "I am perceived more as a minister, professional, and trusted staff person." They are often asked for input in other areas than youth ministry.

The age shift can also change staff structures. The older youth minister may no longer be the youngest person on the staff—the "bottom of the totem pole." In some cases the older youth minister is older than the pastor. While this threatens some senior ministers, most older youth ministers feel more confident in their work. They also report more support for the work done by other staff members.

A Changing Ministry

Youth ministry takes on a different focus for older youth ministers. In response to the question, "Is your ministry different from when you were younger?", there was a unanimous "Yes!" Some indicated their ministry was different because of a difference in today's youth culture, but most indicated a difference because of their own age.

Many of the changes in ministry grow out of the changing relationships with youth and adults. They are more involved with adults—both volunteer leaders and parents of youth. They spend less time with youth and a larger portion of time with the adults who influence youth in a variety of ways. The results usually multiply the number of youth who can be reached by the church's youth ministry. The differing relationships between youth and adults seems to be intentional, not just an automatic response because the youth ministry is growing older.

Another change the older youth ministers reported is in their overall approach to the ministry. Their work is usually more administrative, working through a larger group of people to accomplish goals. They do more planning and have more responsibilities than in earlier years. The activities that are planned have more substance and purpose. Fewer activities are planned just to fill a date on the calendar. By delegating programming responsibilities for smaller events to volunteer youth leaders, the youth minister is able to spend quality time planning for more meaningful events and activities. This also allows the youth minister more time to focus on family and personal needs.

What Would You Do Differently?

If you were starting over, what would you do differently? Most of us have that privilege only in our fantasies. Older youth ministers were asked what suggestions they would offer to younger youth ministers. Their responses can be grouped into five categories of suggestions.

- Put an emphasis on the volunteer youth workers.
- Put an emphasis on your ministry with parents.
- Put an emphasis on discipleship and evangelism.

- Develop counseling skills for youth and adults.
- Learn to integrate youth ministry into the ongoing ministry of the church.

The Quality and Value of Growing Older in Youth Ministry

Growing older in youth ministry is not always a smooth journey. Many youth ministers experience some bumpy segments in the pathway. Mid-life adjustments can be trying experiences.

In response to questions about a mid-life crisis, many older youth ministers reported sensing questions and doubts about staying in youth ministry. About 60 percent said they went through a mid-life crisis, while 40 percent said they had not experienced any serious threats to their self-image. There seems to be no pattern among the ages responding in my survey. Older ones in the group said they had not experienced a mid-life crisis while some younger ones said they had.

The mid-life crisis youth ministers face is not always related to the personal doubts many other adults have. As one youth minister writes, "Very traumatic! Lots of soul searching! Feelings of inadequacy! Questioned my ministry, calling, etc." The youth ministers who reported having doubts about their vocation stated their concerns in four groups.

Some had serious doubts about their changing relationships with youth. One youth minister reports, "Yes, there was a time when I felt I could no longer relate to the needs of the students." They were responding to the adjustments of not being as close to the youth because of the growing difference in their ages.

A second group of concerns related to questions about their continued effectiveness in youth ministry. If they were not as close in age and time spent with youth, could they still be effective in youth ministry? All the youth ministers reported more positive relationships with youth after they worked through their own self-doubts about effectiveness.

A third cluster of concerns dealt with questions about future employment. Some typical statements were, "Will my church continue to value my leadership in youth ministry as I grow older? Will another church call a forty-year-old youth minister? Will I really be leading retreats when I am sixty years old?" Some youth ministers still worry about these concerns and feel like they are venturing into unknown territories in youth ministry.

The fourth group of concerns revolve around the family of youth ministers. Stress and demands of parenting collide with the press of youth ministry needs. Physical changes of middle adulthood require youth ministers to pay more attention to their own energy and well-being. Older youth ministers find it hard to keep up with energetic teenagers. Physical energy is often sapped by youth ministry programming, leaving little time to spend on activities with the family. Salaries of youth ministers may be inadequate to provide for the needs of their own teenagers, especially as they approach the college years. One youth minister writes, "Salary will never be commensurate with what I would like to bring into my family's situation." Older youth ministers are still working through many of these concerns, but with growing confidence that they can face the future with hope.

When asked about future plans, there was an almost unanimous agreement in plans to stay in youth ministry. Over 94 percent said they plan to remain in youth ministry, at least in some form. Some desire additional study in youth ministry and would engage in advanced degrees if the conditions were favorable. Some stated desirable goals as teaching youth ministry in college or seminary, serving in denominational youth positions, or serving as a mentor for a younger youth minister.

I was struck by the deep sense of calling and commitment to youth ministry among older youth ministers. They did not see youth ministry as a stepping stone to something more significant. They did not see themselves as junior ministers or less valuable than others in ministry. Rather, they see themselves serving in a vital, crucial area of ministry that demands the best the church has to offer. Their age is seen as an asset rather than a liability.

Older Youth Ministers as Mentors

Older youth ministers provide an untapped treasure of experiences and wisdom. This body of knowledge about youth ministry could be a valuable asset to those who are younger or less experienced in youth ministry.

When I started as a part-time youth minister in college, I had no one to use as a model for youth ministry. When I was a teenager, our church was small, and we had no one except volunteers to lead the youth ministry. My own parents often sponsored many of the youth activities of our church. I was literally learning youth ministry day by day.

Later I served as a full-time youth minister with little or no training. It did not take long for my shallow cup of experiences to run dry. I remember the first conference I attended in which I met real, live youth ministers who knew something about what they were doing.

I absorbed every word they said. I wrote down names of books they recommended. I asked them questions and marveled at their knowledge and experience. Later, when I attended seminary, the experience of being with those who were wiser and more experienced than I reinforced the value of learning from those who had gone before me in youth ministry.

I still sense these feelings in younger youth ministers across the country and the students I teach in seminary. They are eager to sit with older youth ministers and gain from their knowledge and experience. Older youth ministers also desire ways to share their lives and experiences with younger youth ministers. Why can't these two yearnings be brought together in ways that would benefit all parties concerned?

The model of a mentor comes to mind as an answer to the needs of both older and younger youth ministers. The following are some suggestions for developing a mentoring process in youth ministry.

Seek Out a Mentor

Younger youth ministers should seek out a mentor. An older youth minister in a neighboring church, someone attending a youth ministers' meeting, or a personal acquaintance in youth ministry are likely candidates. Even a fellow staff member who is not a youth minister can be a mentor in many facets of ministry.

Be Available

Older youth ministers should make themselves available. Many older youth ministers serve in churches that employ youth interns. The relationship between older youth minister and intern can be nurtured and blossom into a mentoring relationship with little effort. Seek out younger youth ministers, introduce yourself to them, and make yourself available for fellowship and discussions.

Spend Time Together

Spend time together in social and vocational settings. Mentoring deals with developing skills in a vocation. It also contributes to the broader picture of life. Older youth ministers have much to offer younger ministers, especially as they grow older in ministry. Social settings provide a relaxed time to laugh, enjoy life, and discuss the deeper concerns of all areas of life. Some of my warmest memories grow out of the times my family watched fireworks with a dear friend who is a model of ministry for me.

Develop Lines of Communication

Sometimes a mentor will live some distance from a younger youth minister. It may be difficult to meet face to face except during annual conferences or youth ministers' retreats. However, phone calls and letters can be helpful. Find some mutually convenient ways to talk about youth ministry. Develop the freedom to converse in times of crisis and need.

Provide Markers

Older youth ministers should provide markers. An Ebenezer is usually only an item for a Bible trivia quiz. But it has a deeper meaning in biblical terms (see Gen. 35:14; Josh. 4:9; 24:26; 1 Sam. 7:12). It is a marker that represents an encounter with God or a reminder of God's help along the way.

Markers can be important for youth ministers today. Although we may not pile up stones as a marker, there are other ways of noting significant times in life. A mentor should take note of meaningful accomplishments, a tough problem that was solved, or times of significant growth in spiritual maturity. Mark these with a gift, a word of encouragement, or some physical or symbolic marker to serve as a reminder for years to come. The gift does not have to be expensive to have meaning.

Introduce Younger Youth Ministers

Older youth ministers should introduce younger youth ministers to others in the field. Look for ways to build a network of relationships among youth ministers, youth professionals, and others serving in supportive ways with youth ministry.

Recommend Resources for Growth in Ministry

Older youth ministers may take for granted the books and resources they have at their disposal. Years of service often blur the many small things that have to be learned along the way. Help the younger youth minister by recommending books, other printed materials, films and videos, and guest personalities that may be used in youth ministry. Offer to loan materials that may be out of print.

Accept the Younger Youth Minister as a Peer

The personal qualities of older youth ministers may be their greatest assets. By accepting the younger youth minister as a peer in ministry, you give the younger youth minister more opportunity to observe the personality, attitudes, and outlook of the mentor. Younger youth ministers can help by showing interest in areas of life beyond the tasks of youth ministry. Both should move toward the relationship of mutual interdependence as professionals in youth ministry.

34

Staff Relationships

The horror stories of staff relationships gone sour are rampant. A staff relationship that is warm, supportive, and spiritually vibrant is a joy to the heart. Ministry becomes a daily vocation filled with satisfaction and sense of fulfillment. A staff relationship that is ugly, competitive, and selfish is a torment to the spirit. Ministry becomes a daily task filled with discontent and sense of frustration.

In a recent conference with a group of pastors, some of the comments regarding their associates on the church staff were sobering.

Our minister of youth started dating one of the high school girls. Now she is pregnant, and the whole church is torn up over this incident.

Our minister of music has a group of supporters who always back him in every business meeting. They never want to cooperate with anyone else. The music program operates like it's in a world all by itself.

We had a very good youth minister. However, he never came to staff meetings, never prepared anything on time, only wore jeans to worship services, and ignored the parents. My phone rings off the wall with complaints about him.

On the other hand, I hear horror stories about pastors who are unfaithful, belligerent, and autocratic. Students in seminary classes and youth ministers across the country have shared examples of staff relationships that are filled with anger and strife.

My pastor treats me like a peon. When I try to plan with him, he's always too busy. Then he changes the date for youth activities and announces them from the pulpit without consulting me.

My pastor never supports me when a parent gripes.

We never have staff meetings. I feel like I'm in the dark about what's going on at church.

We planned the youth ministry luncheon for months. It was one of the major events of the year. Then the children's minister planned a family picnic the same day. The minister of education planned another event that conflicted more. How do I win in a situation like that?

The pastor announced that all the staff has to work on Saturday making visits. We don't get a day off during the week. He wants everyone to be a workaholic like him.

Surely God is not pleased with those feelings. Poor staff relationships is a demon that can stifle the work of the Holy Spirit and damage the ministry of an entire church.

Many youth ministers will not be serving in large multistaff churches. There may be only one or two staff members in addition to the pastor. Nevertheless, the potential for conflict still exists.

The relationship with the pastor is the key to a good staff situation for a younger minister. If that relationship is healthy, the youth minister can weather many storms. If that relationship is bad, there is little hope for an effective ministry by that youth minister.

When interviewing with a church, the candidate should have a frank discussion with the pastor. Inquire about his views of youth ministry, expectations about the youth minister's role, and his level of support. Ask about his own plans for the future. Is he preparing to leave or retire soon? Determine his dreams for the church and the role youth ministry plays in those dreams. If the heartbeat of the pastor is resonant with that of the potential youth minister, then a lot of problems will work themselves out along the way.

Building Good Relationships

There are several ways to contribute to good staff relationships. Although none of the following are foolproof, most good staff relationships grow out of the following practices.

Have Regular Staff Meetings

When two or more people work together on common tasks, they need a plan for communicating. A weekly staff meeting offers opportunity for dialogue, planning, and prayer to keep the work going in positive directions.

The staff meeting should include all church workers (including housekeepers, secretaries, and other support staff) in some portion of the meeting. This is a good time for fellowship and prayer. Major church activities on the church calendar can be reviewed at this time.

The ministerial staff could then meet separately to deal with matters in each area of the church's ministry. Calendar planning, problem solving, goal setting, and prayer should be the major work of this portion of the staff meeting.

Convince the Pastor of Your Support

A new staff member presents the possibility of conflict and jealousy. A newer youth minister who draws attention to self rather than to the overall work of the church can be a detriment to the ministry. Some pastors are sensitive about these matters and look for visible evidence of support and loyalty.

The youth minister should work hard to convince the pastor of support and loyalty. It will pay off when the youth minister needs support and loyalty from the pastor.

Overwhelm the Pastor with Information

An irate mother approached the pastor following the morning worship service. "Why can't my son go on the youth mission trip?" The pastor was puzzled and unable to offer a response. He was only vaguely aware of the plans for the trip. When the mother continued to pressure the pastor, he agreed to let the son go on the trip.

Only later did the pastor discover that the son had taken liquor on the last youth trip. Since this trip was a mission project, there were mandatory training sessions. The son had not attended any of the sessions. The youth minister had failed to inform the pastor of any of the plans and requirements of the trip. The result was strained relationships among the pastor, the youth minister, and the boy's mother.

Many youth activities take place away from the church and apart from regular church meetings. This requires a great deal of planning and thought. Since people often look to the pastor for overall leadership of the work of the church, he receives a lot of questions about activities sponsored by the church. The importance of keeping the pastor informed cannot be overemphasized. Especially during the first year of service on a staff, the youth minister should keep the pastor and other staff members informed of youth ministry plans and activities.

Ask for Input from Other Staff Members

When planning for youth ministry, it is helpful to have insight from the perspectives of other people. I once had a supervisor who said, "None of us is as smart as all of us." Other staff members can provide history or background of the church that will assist in planning youth events. By asking for input from others, many problems and conflicts can be avoided and creative ideas will be generated.

Provide Support for Other Staff Members

Some of my best friends in ministry are those with whom I have worked in a church staff position. The fellowship of mutual care and support have built a storehouse of memories to treasure through the years.

Sometimes a person may need to say, "That's not my job," to avoid taking on too many responsibilities. There are occasions when staff members should work alongside others to assist in their areas of responsibilities. A youth minister who willingly helps the music director prepare for a big Christmas music program can enjoy the help the music leader gives during the summer youth camp.

Staff members can also support one another with emotional and personal help during trying times. The prayers of other staff members are gifts from God to help one facing a trial in ministry. Social fellowship among staff members—informal times of fun and relaxation apart from the job—provides a base of emotional support that brings out the best in ministers.

The Pastor's Role in Youth Ministry

Youth ministry is one part of the total ministry of a church. It is an essential part of the connecting link between childhood and adulthood. To ignore the youth ministry is to ignore a vital slice of the life and work of the congregation.

Fran Anderson, a professor who teaches pastoral ministry and youth ministry, observes:

> Pastors have the challenging responsibility and the joyful privilege of giving attention to persons in this life-changing span of years. After thirty-three years in Christian education/youth ministry, I continue to affirm the pastor as the key person to effective youth ministry. This is true even when there is a youth minister on staff.[1]

Obviously, the pastor is a key leader in the church. How can the pastor be closely related to the youth ministry, and still provide the necessary leadership for all the other facets in the life of the church? There is a difference whether the church has a full-time or part-time youth minister (or none at all) and the level of involvement by the pastor. However, the following suggestions for pastors and youth ministers will assist the pastor in the leadership role with youth in the church.

Support and Presence

Youth ministers and pastors both need affirmation, publicly and privately. Everyone appreciates a word of thanks or acknowledgement for a job well done. Critique should be done privately. The goal is to build up the body of Christ (Eph. 4:15-16). The pastor can show support for the youth ministry by attending youth events, even if the visit is short.

During our summer youth camp, the pastor came for one evening. He was there for the afternoon recreation, evening worship, fellowship and watermelon after the service, and devotions before bed time. Although he was there for only one evening, the youth appreciated the fact that he took the time from a busy schedule to be with them. When we returned home, the youth felt like their pastor had something in common with them. The words he spoke from the pulpit about youth camp the following Sunday carried extra weight for the youth group.

Develop Personal Relationships with the Youth

As the youth gathered for Sunday School, they looked up to see the pastor walking their way. The conversation stopped for a moment, until he greeted them and began visiting with the teenagers. A few moments later they were laughing and talking in a relaxed atmosphere. The pastor had begun an important relationship with the teenagers of the congregation.

A few moments spent visiting with youth in the hallway of the church may seem insignificant, but this is important for the youth and for the church. A greeting by the pastor at the door as they arrive communicates warmth and affirmation. A few words spoken in acknowledgment of youth during the sermon says, "You are important. This is your church. We love and care for you."

Help the Pastor Relate to the Youth

This is a way the youth minister can support the pastor in his role with youth. Many pastors do not keep up with the trends in youth culture and feel uncomfortable around teenagers. A youth minister can assist the pastor in knowing how to talk with youth, understand their culture, and relate to them personally.

Pastors often look for good examples to use in sermons. The main problem with sermons, as they pertain to youth, is the lack of positive illustrations relating to youth. The youth ministers can provide positive youth illustrations and examples for the pastor to use. The youth minister can be a link between the youth and pastor and can greatly assist in developing good pastor-youth relationships.

35

Youth Ministry in a Combination Position

People who work with youth also work in numerous other positions of responsibility. A research project with a nation-wide random sample of full-time Southern Baptist youth ministers reveals the following combinations of ministry:[2]

Responsibility	Percent of Total
Youth and Music	42.1
Youth Only	15.7
Youth and Education	14.2
Youth and Recreation	9.7
Other Combinations	18.3

Youth ministers working in combination roles were more often found in churches with membership of 500-749 resident members (31.4 percent were combination and only 4.1 percent had youth responsibilities only). Larger churches (1000-1999 resident members) also had youth ministers working in combination roles (24.9 percent combination and 4.6 percent youth responsibilities only). The following chart shows the size of churches and percentage of each type of youth minister from those responding to the research.[3]

Resident Members	Staff Responsibility	Percent
Under 500	Youth Only	0.5
	Combination	11.7
500-749	Youth Only	4.1
	Combination	31.4
750-999	Youth Only	1.5
	Combination	11.7
1000-1999	Youth Only	4.6
	Combination	24.9
2000 or more	Youth Only	5.1
	Combination	3.5
Size not indicated		1.0

Another survey of youth leaders revealed that youth workers have numerous responsibilities. The following are the ministries included in the work done by those youth ministers:[4]

• High school ministry	89 percent
• Junior high ministry	88 percent
• Counseling	63 percent
• Christian education	56 percent
• Children's ministry	41 percent
• Preaching	38 percent
• College ministry	38 percent
• Young adult ministry	30 percent
• Music ministry	23 percent
• Other	13 percent

Advantages and Disadvantages of Combination Ministry

Being responsible for two or more areas of ministry is an awesome task. Some church staff workers avoid combination ministry while others seek it out with a God-given sense of call.

There are several reasons why combination ministry is popular:

• Many people feel called of God to this type of ministry. They receive their satisfaction from serving in both styles of ministry. They not only enjoy serving in these fields but are successful in them.

• There are many churches which are only large enough to afford one staff member other than the pastor and secretary. Since some fields of ministry, including youth ministry, are specialized fields, a person is needed who is qualified to lead the church in both areas. Therefore the churches seek someone who is capable of doing both jobs.

• One minister may be able to correlate the work of two ministries more effectively. In the combination role of music and youth ministry, it is easier for one person to correlate a program of church music and youth education than for a minister of music and minister of youth to agree upon a program involving both their specialized fields.

Although there are advantages in having one person lead a combination ministry, difficulties are faced when fields are combined:

• Few staff members have qualifications of leadership which make them effective in both fields. It takes a person of unusual abilities to plan and project an adequate youth ministry and at the same time enlist and train leaders in a different program of church ministry. This lack of efficiency in one or both fields may cause some church members who are especially interested in either field to be unhappy with the leadership of the responsible person for both areas.

• Even though staff members are interested in both fields, it is not often that they will take a sufficient amount of time to become properly trained in both fields. Frequently staff members with degrees in church music will take on combined responsibilities. The same is true for those with religious education training. In each case the position calls for specialized training in youth ministry and music. Without the proper balance in training, a minister of music and youth will likely emphasize the area of work he knows best and put less emphasis on the other.

• As the combination ministry increases and becomes more specialized, it becomes almost impossible for a minister to give adequate leadership to both areas of responsibility. The demands can best be met by enlisting and training volunteer leadership. However, it becomes increasingly difficult to maintain growing responsibilities in two different ministries without assistance from additional staff personnel.

A Look at Combination Responsibilities

The combination ministry of music and youth is a common staff position. As a music and youth leader, one must minister in one program to all age groups and in another direction to one age group, cutting through all church program organizations. The following chart shows the arena of responsibilities for a music and youth minister.

Music and Youth Responsibilities

Age Group	Sunday School	Discipleship Training	Music	Missions Education
Adult				
YOUTH				
Children				
Preschool				

Two areas of responsibilities are not shown directly on the chart. These are youth activities (retreats, mission trips, youth council, and so forth) and youth recreation (team sports, drama, puppets, fellow-ships, and so forth). These can be handled best by channeling them through appropriate youth program organizations.

Hints for Two-Hat Wearers

Build Up Your Weak Side

Read books, articles, and current materials related to your weaker side of ministry. Attend conferences and workshops and visit with other church staff who work in the area in which you need help.

Develop the Art of Enlisting and Training Leaders

Delegation is a key survival skill for those working in combination ministries. Key volunteers who are equipped to lead will relieve stress when you are pulled from different directions.

Build Your Ministry Around the Church Program Organizations

This is especially important for youth ministry. Youth ministers who build the strongest, most stable ministry do so as a shared ministry with the youth leaders in the various church program organizations. The youth ministers who are most limited in time and energy are those who try to conduct a "lone ranger" ministry, separate from the church program organizations. They depend on their own ideas and energies. When they move away, the youth ministry often breaks apart because it is not built on a strong foundation of church ministry.

Be Honest in Your Calling

If God has called you to a combination ministry, stay with it. If God has called you to one of the ministries, and you are simply doing the other out of convenience, you will have problems and lack of fulfillment. When the opportunity arises, move into the area of ministry for which God has gifted and equipped you to serve.

Develop "Ad-Ministering" Skills

Administration is a four-letter word to some people. They incorrectly see it as opposed to concern for people. However, administration is working with and through other people. The skills of planning, organizing, executing, supervising, coordinating, publicizing, and evaluating are typical administrative skills. Deficiency in one or more of these skills will make it difficult to work through other people to do ministry.

Part 6
Programming for Youth Ministry

36

Teaching and Learning with Youth

Teaching is more than telling. Teaching is so closely related to learning that the two cannot easily be separated. Teaching can lead to learning, and learning can happen without teaching. However, when there has been no learning, there has not been any teaching.

Active Learning with Youth

Jesus was the perfect teacher. He used many practical methods that can be applied to our teaching with youth. He was actively involved with the disciples in everyday situations. Christ taught them using stories, case studies, parables, object lessons, and examples from their own lives. He used simple objects like coins, water, seeds, and soil to teach profound truths. He engaged them in an active process of learning with Him.

I was teaching a lesson taken from 1 John. I had an outline on the bulletin board, some posters I used for illustrations, a couple of good introductory stories, and an object to illustrate one of the points. I had studied the passage well and outlined each point in detail, but the lesson flopped miserably.

The youth listened at first, then quickly began fidgeting and whispering. Soon, they were talking among themselves or looking bored. I had forgotten one of the most important keys to good teaching/learning with youth: no amount of activity on the part of a teacher will directly result in learning. Learning happens best when the youth are actively involved. Good teaching focuses on finding ways to guide youth to *learn* rather than on finding ways for the teacher to *teach*. What the *student does* is more important than what the *teacher does.*

Research points out the importance of actively involving students in the learning process. Richard Ross studied the activity teaching/learning approach and discovered that active learning is more effective than other methods in changing attitudes of the student.[1]

Although there are too many specific teaching techniques to cover in detail, there are some categories of learning methods that can be briefly mentioned. The following are some categories of learning methods that have proven effective with teenagers. Each category has several methods or techniques of teaching/learning that can be used.

Learning Category	*Examples*
Verbal	Discussion, buzz groups, seminars, question and answer, brainstorming, lecture, reports, panel discussions, and debates
Pencil and Paper	Taking notes, creative writing, paraphrase of Scripture, quizzes, letters, maps, notebooks and puzzles
Art	Posters, montages, stick figures, graffiti wall, murals, banners, illustrating a story, making masks to represent characters or moods, using modeling clay to represent symbols in Scripture, and using cartoons to illustrate a Scripture passage
Music	Background music, analyzing lyrics, writing new lyrics to familiar tunes, writing new tunes to old lyrics, and finding hymn text that paraphrases Scripture
Drama	Role play, acting out Bible stories and events, choral reading, skits, making videos to illustrate a story or truth, simulated TV or radio shows, and acting out a modern parallel to a Bible story
Games	Relays and competition, Bible bowl, variations on TV game shows, and variations on table games Independent Study Work sheets, programmed instruction, assigned readings, research and report projects, and interviews

The Role of Adult Leaders

Two phrases describe the best stance for adults who lead youth in Bible studies: "with youth" and "learning leader." Although there are many qualities that contribute to effective leadership, these form the underlying attitude that makes the difference between success and failure for youth Bible teachers.

Youth Bible study leaders do their best work "with youth." The teacher is a guide who walks alongside youth in the process of discovering God's message to people today. We do our best teaching "with youth" rather than "to youth" or "for youth."

Youth Bible study leaders do their best work as "learning leaders."

The teacher is a colearner in the process. As a partner in the discovery process, we do not relinquish our experiences and knowledge gained from years of study and living. We do admit that we are still "on the way" as lifelong learners in the school of Jesus Christ.

Teaching Youth the Bible

Here is a simple outline for planning a youth Bible study session. This process could be used to prepare for a Sunday morning study, retreat Bible study, weekday study, or anytime you have a study session.

Study the Bible Passages

Read the background passage from several translations. Focus on the selected verses you will deal with in depth. Use the tools you have available—Bible dictionary, Bible atlas, concordance, Bible handbook—to help in your personal study of the passage.

Write a Central Bible Truth

The central Bible truth is a one-sentence statement of the main thrust of the focal passage stated in present tense. This will help you decide the specific learning aim as you continue to plan the lesson.

Consider Youth Needs

Think about the youth who will be in this session. Consider their *felt* needs (the immediate needs they are experiencing at present) and the *perceived* needs (the needs perceived by adults who know and understand the developmental needs of youth) as you continue to prepare. Ask yourself, "What does this central Bible truth have to do with the needs of the youth in my group?"

Select a Teaching Aim

Decide on a specific target for your teaching in this session. Consider what you would like for the youth to be able to do, think, or feel as a result of this study. The teaching aim should be short, simple, and concrete. Pretend you have just finished teaching this session and the youth look at you and say, "OK, now that we've studied this, so what! What do you want me to do about this?" The answer to those statements is the teaching aim.

Select Bible Learning Activities

Jot down several Bible learning activities that could be used in this session. Use a variety of creative, active learning methods. Selecting Bible learning activities is like using a road map. The teaching aim is your destination and the Bible learning activities is your route to get there. You may take several routes, but the important object is to arrive at the destination. Arrange the Bible learning activities in the following order:

● *Focus attention.*—Plan at least one activity to grab their attention and help youth focus their thoughts on the central Bible truth of the lesson.

● *Dig into the Scriptures.*—Plan for activities to actively involve youth in digging into God's Word to discover for themselves the truths and principles there.

● *Guide the application.*—Plan for one or two activities to help youth make application of the biblical truths to their own lives. Try to avoid saying, "Here's how this lesson applies to your life. . . ." Instead, allow time for brainstorming and planning ways to put the study into practice in concrete, specific ways during the following week.

37

Discipling Youth

What Is Discipleship?

The word *discipleship* often triggers a variety of images in the minds of youth leaders. Some will think of one-to-one discipleship, while others think of new Christian follow up, small-group discipleship, a discipleship notebook, a group of committed Christians growing in mutual accountability, or a pastor teaching a series of Bible studies to the congregation.

Discipleship is more than a program or process. Ultimately, discipleship is a relationship with Jesus Christ. It also involves fellowship with believers in the context of a local church and expressing faith through words and deeds to unbelievers outside the body of Christ.

> Discipleship is the Christian's lifelong commitment to the person, teaching, and spirit of Jesus Christ. Life under Jesus' lordship involves progressive learning, growth in Christlikeness, application of biblical truth, responsibility for sharing the Christian faith, and responsible church membership.[2]

Leading a Discipleship Group

I invited David, a sophomore in high school, to help me lead some discipleship sessions with our youth group. We planned ways to share the leadership of the group each week. He gradually assumed more leadership as the sessions progressed. When we finished the study, I was disappointed because I thought the discussions were shallow and the youth did not show much spiritual growth.

The following spring, David was selected to be the pastor during a week of emphasis on youth in the church. He was to preach during a youth-led service on Sunday night. As he nervously began, I recognized the points in his sermon. They were the titles of the sessions in the discipleship study we had done several months earlier.

When David was called on to express his faith in public, he looked to his earlier experience of shared leadership for help. I learned a valuable lesson in leadership. Youth can gain as much from their experience of leadership as they gain from the content of the lessons we teach.

Shared leadership involves youth in active leadership of a group. Youth and adults plan and lead sessions of study together. The experience of sharing leadership with adults helps youth to feel ownership of the group and teaches a worthwhile lesson in leadership.

Leading a discipleship group is a little different from leading a Bible study session. There is a need for more group building and mutual disclosure among the members. Accountability grows as group members feel increasingly closer to each other in their growth toward Christlikeness. This process can be helped by following some principles of leadership.

- *Plan an arrival activity.*—Select one or two icebreakers to add warmth and congeniality to the session. Ideally these activities should point toward the goal of the session.

- *Build group spirit.*—Use one or more approaches to build the spirit of the group. Sharing prayer requests, talking about the events of the past few days, checking up on progress toward personal goals, or asking members about personal spiritual progress are some ways to do this.

- *Use shared leadership.*—Involve the youth in planning and leading the learning experience.

- *Allow time for personal discussion and interaction.*—Plan ways to involve members in exploring the biblical truths of the discipleship session.

- *Plan for application.*—Explore ways to put the new learning into practice as soon as possible. Individual and group plans may need to be developed. If this involves a new skill, time should be allowed to practice the new skill.

- *Make assignments and commitments.*—Allow time to clarify the assignments before the next meeting. Select some way for group members to make a commitment to carry out the assignments.

Types of Discipleship

Discipleship can take more than one form. Paul used one-on-one approaches (Acts 16:1-3; Phil. 2:19-22), group training (Acts 11:26), letter writing (1 Tim.; Titus), and preaching (Acts 17:16). Barnabas had a remarkable gift of encouragement (4:36; 9:26-28). Aquila and Priscilla used their home as a base of devotion and encouragement for Paul (18:1-4) and a place of instruction for Apollos (vv. 24-26).

Jesus used several approaches to discipleship training with His disciples. We often think of the ministry with the twelve as Jesus' only method of discipling. He did spend large blocks of time with the small group of dedicated followers in training, fellowship, prayer, and ministry. He also spent significant amounts of time with three members of the group—Peter, James, and John. In addition, Peter and John received special attention from Jesus. Jesus also related to the masses as He taught them (Matt. 5—7 and Luke 6), performed miracles (Mark 1:32-33), and provided food for the five thousand (Matt. 14:13-21).

Jesus approached discipleship in at least three levels—the five thousand (masses), the twelve (small groups), and with individuals within these groups (one-on-one). These three types of discipleship training offer a framework for youth discipleship training today.

Some type of discipleship training should be offered for the masses in the youth group. *On-going discipleship training* designed to be appealing and instructive for all youth fits this approach. Sunday evening discipleship groups, with a group for every youth, using suitable study materials and led by dedicated youth leaders, fit this model.

Specialized, *short-term discipleship studies or learning experiences* should be offered for smaller groups within the youth group. These studies can meet special needs or interests and provide selective discipleship training for those ready to grow more spiritually. A series of Sunday night seminars, a week-long study, retreats, discipleship courses, and camps provide the settings for this approach to discipleship training.

One-on-one discipleship is the third type of discipleship training. This meets the need for individual attention in some youth and provides excellent follow-up for new Christians. Youth who have special commitments for vocational Christian service can benefit from a one-on-one relationship as an apprentice with a mentor in ministry.

38

Tasting the Joy of Service

The music softly played as youth went to each other, one by one, to offer thanks for the joy of their friendship and fellowship. The words of Scripture had just recalled the last night Jesus was with His disciples. He had given an example of servant leadership by washing the disciples' feet. We were having our last devotional time at the end of our mission trip. The joy of this service was fresh and sweet.

The Great Commission (Matt. 28:18-20) tells us to be involved in making disciples around the world, teaching them to be obedient to the words and example of Jesus. He promises His presence and authority to carry out this command. He also promises blessings and joy (John 13:17) if we follow Him in faithful service.

Many of the activities of youth ministry promise a good time and fellowship. Most of the activities are designed to *give youth something*. Seldom do we ask youth to *give of themselves* in ministry and service. Mission activities and projects are some of the best ways for youth to give rather than receive.

The thrill of social activities soon passes. However, the joy that comes from faithful service to God lingers long past the fading memories of fellowships, parties, and banquets.

Why We Need Missions Education

Missions education offers values beyond the reach of other programs of youth education. There are at least four values of a well-rounded missions education approach in youth ministry.

First, a missions education program builds balanced disciples. The Bible study program helps youth to know the Word of God. The discipleship training groups help youth apply the Word of God in daily lives. A missions education program helps youth be and do what God commands through His Word.

Second, a missions education program helps to grow future missionaries. Knowledge usually precedes a call to service. God can work better in a mind that is aware of the missions opportunities for service at home and abroad. Most missionaries I have known sensed a call to missions while they were active members of a missions education group in church.

Third, a missions education program helps youth grasp a world view. On a recent mission trip to Central America, youth witnessed extreme poverty, hunger, sickness, and deplorable living conditions. Most of the youth had never seen how the world lives outside their own comfortable surroundings. When they returned home, another teenager was complaining because she did not have a new school wardrobe. One of the youth who had been on the mission trip responded, "You have all you need!"

Finally, a missions education program equips youth to serve in other areas of ministry. Missions is a *giving* rather than *receiving* operation.

Helping Youth Reach Beyond Their World

Adolescents tend to be self-centered. A high school girl has a hard time thinking beyond her school. Her time is devoted to relating to friends, classes, teachers, and activities of the immediate world. She will need guidance to broaden her vision to the entire world. Missions education can be the catalyst for youth to catch a vision for reaching their world for Christ.

Acts 1:8 promises power through the Holy Spirit to reach around the world in witnessing for Christ. Jesus specifically commanded His followers to be witnesses in "Jerusalem, and in all Judea and Samaria, and even to the remotest part of the earth."

We are to be witnesses in our immediate surroundings (Jerusalem) and the areas nearby (Judea). We are also to be witnesses in the areas that are hard to penetrate (Samaria). For a high school study, Samaria may be the parts of the school that are difficult for some students to enter. It may be hard for an member of the Latin Club to hang out in the agriculture building. A member of the Thespians may not feel comfortable wandering into the field house with the athletes. The president of the band may not want to associate with the group of students who meet across the street and smoke during lunch. Samaria may be real to contemporary high school students.

We are also commanded to witness around the world, even to the remotest parts of the earth. How can a teenager do this? Is this something only mature adults can do? Youth can literally reach around the world through prayer and support for mission efforts, if they are encouraged to do so. A missions education program can provide the channel for witnessing at home, in the surrounding state, in cities, in our country, and even around the whole earth.

Examples of Mission Projects

Youth should be able to learn about missionaries and missions work of the church and denomination. They should be familiar with individual missionaries and the various ways to do missions. Youth should be aware of the possibility that God could call them into full-time vocational mission service as well as a volunteer or in short-time service.

Youth can be actively involved in a variety of missions activities. Mission trips, missions/ministry projects, and addressing social and moral needs are examples of missions involvement for youth.

Mission Trips and Projects

Many churches plan an annual youth mission trip. Backyard Bible Clubs, vacation Bible schools, choir performances, puppet performances, revivals, door-to-door surveys, and work projects are activities done on such trips. The same type activities may be done in a local setting.

Ministry/Mission Projects

Many mission activities could be planned for the local community. A distinction between *ministry* and *missions* activities is helpful. *Ministry projects* have to do with people who are members or immediate prospects of the local church. *Mission projects* have to do with people who are beyond the bounds of the church membership. In a well-developed youth ministry, ministry actions are best carried out through the Sunday School or Bible teaching program. Mission projects are more closely related to the missions education organization.

Some examples of the types of ministry that could be performed (either to members or nonmembers) are: delivering flowers to shut-ins, visiting elderly people in a nursing home, repairing homes for elderly, teaching English as a second language to ethnic groups, providing a tutoring program for inner-city children, and leading a recreational Bible study meeting after school where there is no church nearby.

Addressing Social and Moral Needs

Social and moral issues confront us daily. Youth can find immediate ways to apply biblical teachings to meet such needs. Some examples of mission projects in this area are: providing food and shelter for the homeless, operating a food pantry for hungry people, leading various recreational programs for inner-city youth, working in projects related to hungry people around the world or environmental concerns, and working to combat immoral issues on a local basis.

39

Saturating Youth Ministry with Evangelism

Youth ministry is much more than fun and games. It is also more than serious, no-frills, intense Bible study. We must seek a balance in order to attract youth to the message of hope in Jesus Christ.

Evangelism is too often approached as a separate program that has to coexist with other activities of youth ministry. Rather than setting evangelism aside as a concern to address from time to time, it should be the seasoning that flavors all we do in youth ministry. Evangelism should permeate every program, activity, and emphasis in youth ministry.

Youth ministry without evangelism is like a robot going through mechanical routines. With no life or energy of its own, a robot mindlessly performs the tasks assigned and programmed. Youth ministry can function as efficiently as a machine, but without evangelism it is just going through the motions.

Discipleship and evangelism go hand in hand. They are difficult to separate because of the nature of the two. Discipleship that does not lead toward evangelism is not true Christian discipleship. Evangelism that does not grow out of discipleship is simply actions performed as a duty.

Jesus-Style Evangelism

Which is more important in youth evangelism: developing personal relationships or delivering the message of salvation? Jesus approached evangelism from several directions. He used different styles of communicating the truth about Himself, with varying levels of personal relationship and amount of content in the message.

We will consider five styles of evangelism found in the earthly ministry of Jesus. The following chart illustrates these five styles and the corresponding degree of personal relationship or content in the approach He used.

JESUS STYLE EVANGELISM

Relational	Environmental	Presentational	Informational
Wedding at Cana	Woman at the Well Nicodemus	Banquet—"Compel them to come in"	Sermon on the Mount Mark 1:33 "the whole city was at the gate"

←——— Prayer for Spiritual Awakening (John 17) ———→

RELATIONSHIPS

CONTENT

Relational

At the wedding in Cana of Galilee (John 2:1*ff.*), Jesus helped an embarrassed host when the wine ran out. This first miracle was a small glimpse of the glory of Jesus. The level of personal relationships was high (He was a guest at a party), and the level of the content was low, but there was still an element of evangelism. His disciples believed in Him because of this incident (v. 11).

Relational evangelism can be employed in youth ministry through fellowships, informal contacts in social settings, refreshment times during group meetings, and through a variety of youth socials.

Environmental

Jesus had a unique ability to communicate the gospel in the language of the environment. This can be seen clearly in His encounter with the Samaritan woman at the well and in the night meeting with Nicodemus.

In John 3, Nicodemus came to Jesus with questions about spiritual matters. Although Nicodemus was a leader among the Pharisees, John says he came to Jesus *by night,* indicating not only that it was after sundown but that Nicodemus was in spiritual darkness. Jesus told Nicodemus he had to be "born again" to see the kingdom of God (v. 3). Nicodemus, a well-schooled Pharisee, knew his family heritage backward and forward. He had kept the laws of Jewish tradition faithfully. Jesus said, in effect, "Nicodemus, you have to get a new family tree. You must be born again into a new kind of family."

On another occasion, in John 4, Jesus passed through Samaria in order to meet a woman at the city well (vv. 4-7). Jesus took the initiative and asked for a drink from the Samaritan woman. By doing so Jesus crossed barriers of race, tradition, religion, and the contemporary society to witness to the woman. During the conversation, Jesus offered her "living water" (v. 10). This broke through all facades to touch the woman's greatest need. She was an outcast because of her life-style. The other women of the city did not allow her to come to the well with them. Water was a daily reminder of her hopeless condition. Living water offered the hope for a new life.

Why did Jesus not use the term "living water" with Nicodemus? Why did Jesus not talk to the Samaritan woman about being "born again?" Jesus used the language of the environment to communicate the message of salvation. He used the language that communicated best with each person.

Jesus used the language of the environment to focus on personal relationships and increase the level of gospel content. Environmental evangelism can be seen in youth ministry in helping teenagers learn to speak of their faith in everyday terms. How would a teenager witness to an athlete, a computer hacker, a political science whiz, or a musician? Beginning with a personal testimony, help youth discover ways to talk about their faith as freely as they talk about food, movies, sports, and cars.

Presentational

Jesus told a parable about a rich man who gave a banquet that no one attended (Luke 14:16ff). All the invited guests gave excuses why they could not attend. So the rich man instructed his servants to go into the highways and hedges and "compel them to come in" (v. 23).

There is a time when we need to impress upon people the urgency of responding to Jesus Christ. The personal relationship is still evident in this style of evangelism, but the degree of content in the message is higher than other styles.

This approach to evangelism is often seen in personal evangelism methods. Using witnessing tracts, memorizing an outline of the Gospel plan of salvation, and learning ways to initiate a witnessing conversation are examples of this style of evangelism. Youth can learn a simple outline such as the Roman Road (Rom. 3:23; 5:8; 6:23; 10:9-10) or other familiar outlines to explain how to become a Christian.

Informational

Jesus spoke to the masses on several occasions. The Sermon on the Mount (Matt. 5—7) and the feeding of the five thousand (John 6:1ff) are two examples of this style of evangelism with the masses. The level of interpersonal relationships is low and the message or content is high.

This style of evangelism is often called mass evangelism. Youth can be involved in this style evangelism through youth rallies, after-game fellowships, youth revivals, youth camps and retreats, and youth choir presentations.

Prayer

In the High Priestly prayer of John 17, Jesus prayed for all the disciples through the ages, asking for power and sanctification as they take the message of salvation to all the world. We are all included in this prayer. We can follow this model by praying for all people to be won to Christ.

When a person makes a public profession of faith, the pastor presents the person to the church and invites everyone to come and extend a welcome. Youth often move on with little attention to the new

Christian. However, when the person is a teenager for whom several in the youth group have been praying, there is a different reaction. The youth group will crowd around with tears and smiles, hugging, laughing, and rejoicing with the new Christian in their midst. The difference is in the level of investment in evangelism through prayer.

Youth may not be actively engaged in all styles of evangelism. Some youth may find it hard to take a witnessing tract and initiate a conversation with a stranger. Others may participate in few or none of the different styles of evangelism. All Christian youth can be engaged in prayer for their lost friends. This is the bottom line in evangelism. Prayer is the beginning point and the source of motivation for all we do in youth evangelism.

Encourage youth to pray for lost friends in their Sunday School classes, discipleship groups, and other classes at church. Help them keep personal prayer lists of lost friends. Remind the youth to pray regularly for friends who are not Christians and people around the world to come to know Christ.

40

Recreation in Youth Ministry

The bus pulled out of the church parking lot loaded with teenagers headed for youth camp. I looked around at the faces of my new youth group and wondered how to get to know all these people. Since coming to this church only a few days earlier, I had visited with just a few in the group. We still smiled and greeted each other politely but did not feel very well acquainted.

The first few events at youth camp were stiff and formal. When I spoke before the group, I felt like a stranger. As we played volleyball and softball, ate together at meals, went on hikes in the afternoons, laughed together at fellowship times, and quietly sang around the campfires, the walls between us went down, and we grew to be close friends. The difference was recreation.

Youth ministry is more than fun and games. However, youth ministry without fun and games is like eating cold pizza and a month-old soda—the basic ingredients are there, but the warmth and fizz are gone. Too little recreation in youth ministry leads to a lack of sparkle and vitality.

Balance in Youth Ministry

Recreation is an important element when it exists in balance with other elements of youth ministry. The proper role of recreation is as *support* to the other programs of youth ministry. As discussed in Part 1, recreation can be balanced when it is channeled through the church program organizations. An after-church fellowship sponsored by a Sunday School class or department becomes an extension of the Bible teaching and outreach effort of the youth ministry. It is more than just another fellowship.

Recreation that exists apart from the ongoing program organizations must be constantly monitored to see if there is a balance between fun and serious events. On the other hand, recreation that is linked as closely as possible to the other youth program organizations will achieve balance by supporting the Bible teaching, discipleship, music, and missions education efforts of the church.

Examples of Recreation

Several types of recreation can be scheduled. Each of the following types has a variety of activities associated with it.

● *Social recreation*—parties, games, fellowships, banquets, receptions, meals, and refreshments.

● *Sports and games*—outdoor sports, indoor and outdoor games, organized leagues, quiet games, table games, icebreakers, and get-acquainted activities.

● *Camping*—summer camps, stress camping, adventure and wilderness camping, backpacking, and day hiking.

● *Retreats*—weekend retreats, prayer and renewal retreats, lock-ins, home retreats, planning retreats, and day retreats.

● *Arts, crafts and hobbies*—seminars and classes, craft and hobby fairs, arts festivals, and informal discussions related to hobbies.

● *Aerobics and fitness*—fitness classes and aerobics workouts.

● *Drama*—play productions, puppets, audiovisual presentations, skits, role plays, fun drama, monologues, choral readings, and storytelling.

● *Therapeutic recreation*—recreation designed to be inclusive of those with physical handicaps, special olympics, and recreation for those recovering from injuries.

The Value of Camps and Retreats

Jesus often went aside with His disciples for periods of prayer and refreshment. He used these times for teaching, relaxation, fellowship, and prayer. These retreats gave the disciples occasion to reflect on their commitment and the chance to grow deeper in their understanding and devotion.

Camps and retreats provide the same opportunities for youth ministry today. They set the stage for prayer, teaching, deeper understanding of discipleship, evangelism, and commitment. A youth may learn more in a few days of reflection, study, and commitment at youth camp than in weeks of normal routines back home. Through campfire worship times, outdoor education, trust-building exercises, creative study and worship, and special memories of camps or youth retreats, youth come to know Jesus in a special way. The memories of fellowship and spiritual growth with other youth and adults hold a special place in the minds of teenagers who participate in these activities.

Plan Retreats with Purpose

Planning for retreats falls into two general categories: calendar planning and planning the retreat schedule.

Calendar planning involves choosing the appropriate time during the year for retreats. Retreats should be planned to fit the overall youth ministry calendar for the year. Do not plan a retreat simply because there is a school holiday or because a retreat was scheduled at that particular time last year. Plan retreats to meet goals and purposes, not to fill a calendar space.

The schedule for a retreat should be well planned before the retreat begins. I heard a youth minister say, "We don't have anything planned for our retreat. We're just going to get away for the weekend and relax." The fifty-plus youth going on that retreat had some plans in mind, and they were not the plans the youth minister expected!

Retreats can be well-planned and still leave unstructured free times. Retreats are excellent times for creative worship and learning experiences. Blocks of time should be scheduled for Bible study, worship, recreation, free time, fellowship, and other discussions. Allow time for preparation for meals and bedtimes.

Youth Camps

Youth camps can be planned by one church or a group of churches. Most often a youth camp is a week-long summer activity designed to attract and appeal to a large number of youth members and prospects. Several churches, an association, or an organization, can usually plan a more fully developed camp program. Larger churches, however, can plan an entire camp schedule specifically tailored to meet their needs.

Youth camps fall into two general categories: centralized and decentralized. A centralized camp is planned to pull together the entire group for worship, Bible study, fellowship, and recreation. In this camp program, a church would participate with other churches in common experiences of worship, Bible study, recreation, campfire programs, meals, and fellowships. Individual church groups may also have some times for meeting with their own youth.

A decentralized camp allows each entity (church group, grade, or other groupings) to conduct many of the Bible study and worship experiences, meals, and fellowship times. A decentralized camp, for example, would plan for individual church groups to lead their own Bible studies, fellowships, meals, and recreation. Some large group experiences—worship, campfire, meals, and recreation—may still be planned for the entire camp group.

Youth camps may be situated in a variety of locations. Residential encampments provide an ideal setting for youth camp. Camps may also be located in college dorms, at state parks, at the church, at a weekend cabin, and in homes.

41

Planning to Meet Needs

Planning with Purpose

Planning is a necessary part of any endeavor. Even those activities that are "unplanned" require some preparation, which may be done while the activity progresses. In the past, youth ministers were stereotyped as impetuous, free-flowing, impulsive, and spontaneous. With reckless abandon they launched into activities. This often resulted in poorly planned youth activities and poor support for youth ministry.

Today many youth ministers see the benefits of planning. Activities and events deserve the thought and preparation that leads to quality rather than haphazard happenings. Some general guidelines will aid in this planning process.

First, plan activities with purpose. Do not plan an event simply because it was planned in the past, unless that event or activity meets a purpose or need. A youth minister who changed churches almost every year once said he had been in youth ministry ten years. In reality, he had been in youth ministry only one year; he had just done it ten times!

Second, plan youth ministry to meet the needs of your group. A youth group in Texas is different from a group in New England. A group in Florida is quite different from a youth group in the mountains of Colorado. Programming for inner-city or rural youth calls for activities to meet different needs from those of suburban youth. Take a serious look at the spiritual, economic, social, and family needs of the youth group before scheduling activities or events.

Finally, activities should grow out of overarching goals and objectives. A well-planned youth ministry will have a cohesiveness and sense of purpose. Too often a youth ministry calendar looks like a collection of unrelated activities with no purpose other than keeping youth too busy to sin. Activities will be related to each other and will move toward a common goal.

Steps in the Planning Process

Well-planned youth ministry does not just happen. It takes a level of thought and cooperation among several people for a balanced youth ministry to fall into place. The following steps will help plan a comprehensive youth ministry for a church.[3]

Evaluate

Take a serious look at the way things are at present. Seek input from youth, parents, church staff, volunteer leaders of youth, and other interested persons. Determine the strengths and weaknesses of the total youth ministry.

Select Priorities

Use the information gained during the evaluation process to identify and select some priorities for the youth ministry. What kinds of things need to be improved? What areas do we need to strengthen? What activities or programs do we need to continue or develop? These questions will help in selecting priorities.

Determine Goals

Most goals will grow out of the priorities selected. Some goals may be related to churchwide emphases or denominational goals. Choose your goals wisely, because they will become the stackpoles for planning the entire youth ministry.

Goals are the clearly defined areas which you will work toward during the time frame of the planning period. Include a broad cross section of youth, parents, and leaders in the goal-setting process so that the goals become *our goals.* Goals should be stated in such a way as to be measurable, achievable, and observable.

List Actions to Reach the Goals

The goals will not happen without purposeful actions. Brainstorm activities, events, studies, and emphases to move toward the goals. Gather ideas from as many persons in the youth ministry as practical. Read books, use ideas from other youth ministers, and list your own ideas based on your knowledge of the youth group.

Channel the ideas through the youth program organizations as much as possible. You may not be able to use all the ideas. This is not important at this stage.

Develop a Tentative Calendar

Put churchwide events on the calendar, especially those that involve youth. List all activities planned by the youth program organizations. List seasonal emphases and look for ways to use these as some of the youth ministry events. Consider balance, variety, age groups involved, and timing of activities. Major school events that involve your youth should also be considered.

Gather Feedback and Refine the Calendar

This step will help avoid some problems of conflicts with other church or community activities. Share the tentative calendar with key persons in the youth ministry. All church staff members should review the calendar to spot potential conflicts. It is not necessary for all youth, parents, or youth leaders to see the tentative calendar. Representative groups should see the calendar and offer suggestions for refinements. This will sharpen the planning and involve more people in a sense of ownership of the youth ministry. Involving people at this stage of the planning also serves to promote the youth activities on the calendar.

All suggestions and refinements cannot be made on the calendar. However, consider all suggestions and use as many as possible. Print the calendar in final form and distribute to the youth group, parents, youth leaders, and other interested persons.

Use the Calendar for Budget Planning and the Budget for Calendar Planning

Youth ministers must learn to work with the resources the church has available for youth ministry. Plan your budget to meet the needs of the programs and activities for the coming year. However, if your budget does not allow for ten major youth events next summer, do not put ten major events on the calendar.

A Process for Ongoing Planning

Once the calendar planning is finished, the real work begins. Youth ministry does not just happen, even if it is planned well. It takes a process of continual planning and coordination to bring about the activities, emphases, and events on the youth ministry calendar.

Planning with Youth

The youth burst out of the van and headed for the cabin to claim bunks and scout out the location. After an afternoon of recreation and hot dogs, we settled in for a weekend of prayer and planning. When we left the cabin the next day, we had some general plans for the youth calendar for the coming year.

Excitement and motivation grows when youth are involved in the

planning process. We made several exciting plans during the weekend planning retreat. It took all year long to bring the ideas into reality.

Youth can and should be involved in the planning process. They can
participate in the overall planning of the youth ministry calendar as
well as the planning for a specific event. This involvement develops
leadership and teaches responsibility. The youth ministry council (see
chapter 42) is a good vehicle for this ongoing planning.

Planning with Youth Leaders

An effective, biblical youth ministry equips youth leaders for the
work of ministry. Each adult will see his or her role as a coleader in
ministry with youth. This takes an approach of mutual planning and
sharing to work in coordination and avoid competition and conflicts.

Youth leaders in the different church program organizations will
need to plan for their respective areas on a regular basis. Youth Sunday School leaders, for example, should meet weekly for planning and
preparation of the Sunday morning Bible study and other related work.

All the youth leaders need to meet on a regular basis for fellowship,
goal setting, and detailed calendar planning. A quarterly planning
meeting is helpful for this work. If the group of leaders is large, a meal
at the church followed by a planning time may work best. Allow time
for reports and for each group of leaders to share plans for their division of the youth ministry. Discuss churchwide events and major youth
projects that require planning across program organization lines.

Planning with Parents

The pies were sliced, the coffee was brewing, and parents of youth
were gathering at the home of one of the members. It was our quarterly "Talk-Back" for parents of youth in the church. It was a good time of
fellowship among the parents. We also spent some time reviewing the
youth events of the past three months and looked forward to the activities in the months ahead. Parents had a chance to voice concerns
and share ideas about the direction of the youth ministry.

Parents have hopes and dreams for their teenagers. When the
youth ministry of the church encourages parents in their efforts, it can
be a successful team. However, when parents feel the youth ministry
ignores their hopes and dreams, it can be frustrating. A wise youth
minister will seek ways to gain input from parents concerning the direction and plans of the youth ministry.

A parent council can help in the ongoing planning for parents. Select a group of parents to meet regularly (every month if possible) to
discuss plans for the youth parents of the church. This group can also
function as a sounding board for ideas for future youth events.

Planning with Other Church Staff

Regular meeting times with other church staff aids in the ongoing planning process. If your church has a regular staff meeting, this is a good time to coordinate the youth ministry plans with those of other areas of ministry.

Long-range planning by the church staff is quite helpful, especially in the early stages of planning for the youth ministry calendar. It can be disconcerting to plan the entire youth ministry calendar, print and distribute the calendars, and then discover that a major churchwide event has been scheduled at the same time as a major youth activity. A staff planning retreat affords the opportunity for goal setting, coordination, and long-range calendar planning.

Planning can also take place in informal, unstructured meetings between church staff members. A youth minister might meet with the music minister, for example, to discuss plans for the youth choir and the youth mission trip. The youth minister and children's minister might brainstorm ways to help other children prepare for adolescence and feel welcome into the youth group.

42

The Youth Ministry Council

Involving Youth in Planning

Planning for youth ministry should involve youth. This has been a practice from the earliest eras of youth ministry. Today youth can be involved in a variety of ways and degrees of responsibility. The youth ministry council is a prime vehicle for this process.

Some youth groups may not need a youth ministry council. Smaller youth groups may not need to select youth to represent the whole group. There are some advantages and disadvantages to having a planning council selected from the youth group.

One disadvantage to having a youth council is that it may become a clique and plan only for the members of the group. Youth with potential for leadership and ministry may be left off the planning council. A problem can arise when the youth council begins to plan activities with no relationship to the church program organizations. The result is a youth ministry separate from the ongoing work of the church.

An advantage of the youth council is the unity that grows as youth plan and work together. Relationships between youth and adults can be enhanced as they work together on projects and plans. In a large youth group, the youth council can bring together the different groupings toward some common goals and activities. Other advantages of the youth council lie in the deeper insight of ministry as youth serve the church by planning for the total youth ministry.

Models of Youth Councils and Committees

The older model of planning used by some churches is a youth council made up of youth and a youth committee made up of parents. A recurring problem with this approach was that the youth council planned something and the youth committee vetoed it.

Some churches still use this structure. Youth are selected from Bible study classes, different groups in the church, or different grades. This youth council then meets to plan social and recreational activities and major projects for the youth group.

The youth committee as used by some churches is a standing committee of adults. The youth committee normally does not plan programs, although it may be involved in establishing guidelines and policy.

A better model for planning with youth and adults is the Youth Ministry Council. This is a balanced group of youth, parents, and volunteer youth leaders. This structure provides a blend of the old youth council and youth committee formats for better planning in youth ministry.

Youth members of the Youth Ministry Council can be selected in a variety of ways. Youth may be nominated and elected by popular vote. A better way is to have youth complete applications for membership on the Youth Ministry Council. A team of youth leaders and the youth minister can then screen and select the youth representatives.

Adults on the Youth Ministry Council consist of youth leaders and parents of youth. Key youth leaders from the church program organizations (Sunday School department directors, the youth choir director, and so forth) may automatically become members. If some of these youth leaders are not parents of youth, representative parents should be enlisted to be a part of the group.

A balanced group of youth and adults is important. Do not overpower the youth with adult members. The ideal structure is a team of youth and adults who feel accepted and respected as partners in planning.

Using the Youth Ministry Council

Most social, recreational, and ministry activities should be channeled through the church program organizations. Even major projects can be broken down and assigned to appropriate programs for planning and implementation. So where does this leave the Youth Ministry Council? How does this group relate to the total youth ministry?

These are important questions that must be understood if the Youth Ministry Council is to function effectively. The Youth Ministry Council provides an ideal environment for pulling together the different elements of youth ministry for brainstorming, goal setting, and mutual support. The plans made by individual classes and departments can be shared with the Youth Ministry Council for monthly planning. This will avoid a calendar that is too busy or too empty. Youth will gain a comprehensive picture of the total youth ministry.

Finally, the Youth Ministry Council can assist in preparing a budget for the church's youth ministry. The makeup of the Youth Ministry Council consists of youth and adults from a cross section of the church body. This will also lend credibility to the recommendations to the budget-planning committee of the church.

43

Budgeting for Youth Ministry

"Budget planning is not hard for my youth ministry. We don't get any!" Predicaments like the one faced by this young youth minister can be avoided with proper budget planning. Even when no money is collected for youth ministry from the overall church budget, some funds are necessary to carry on programming. A good plan for budgeting could lead to more financial support from the church body.

Ministry-Based Budgeting

The budget planning process begins with a good calendar planning process. Calendar plans that grow out of goals and priorities related to spiritual growth will reflect a ministry-based approach to youth ministry. A church is more likely to underwrite such an approach. Many churches balk at providing funds for a youth ministry that is simply based on a series of social activities.

The events, emphases, and activities on the youth ministry calendar should be listed and grouped according to areas within the youth ministry. Such groupings could include youth leader development, parent ministry, youth camp, outreach and evangelism, ministry and mission projects, literature, general recreation, socials and fellowships, and program organization support.

Investigate costs and project expected expenditures for each item on the youth ministry calendar. Estimate the amount youth will pay for some events such as youth camp, retreats, or banquets. Plan to cover the costs for adult chaperons whenever possible.

Include the Youth Ministry Council in the budget planning process. Use this input to set fees for major events such as youth camp or mission trips. Seek input from significant leaders in the church about youth ministry budgets in the past. Use these figures in planning a realistic budget for the church.

Prioritize the budget to allow for the possibility of less money than desired. Some activities and events might have to be cut from the budget if too little money is available. By basing the budget on ministry goals rather a lump sum of money, a budget planning committee will see that when money is cut, the result is a cut in the ministry of the church.

Finally, be flexible. Some other areas of the church's ministry may need funds more than the youth ministry. During times when funds are less, everyone has to adapt. Willingness to be flexible can help in the future when greater needs arise in youth ministry.

Sample Budget Form

Work sheets for actions, emphases, and areas of ministry can be used to gather information about costs and determine basic financial needs. See the sample form which is provided.

The recommendation to the church budget planning committee should be a summary of the work sheet information, grouped into the budget areas mentioned earlier. The following is a sample format:

1. *Youth Leadership Development*
- *Youth Leader Retreat*　　　　　$xxx

To provide a retreat for all youth leaders for training, goal setting, and fellowship. This relates to the ministry goal of leadership development.
- *Potential Leader Training*　　　　$xx

To purchase supplies for a potential leader training course. This relates to the ministry goal of outreach.

TOTAL　　　　　　　　　　　$XXX

2. *Youth Camps and Retreats*
- *Youth Camp*　　　　　　　　$xxxx

To cover costs of sponsors' fees, promotion, transportation, insurance, food, and lodging. Youth will be charged $xx per person to offset costs. This relates to the ministry goals of outreach and spiritual development.
- *Spring Retreat*　　　　　　　$xxx

To cover costs of sponsors' fees, promotion, transportation, lodging, food, and program personnel. This relates to the ministry goal of discipleship training.

(Continue with remaining items in the youth ministry budget.)

TOTAL　　　　　　　　　　　$XXX

BUDGET WORKSHEET

YOUTH PROGRAM ORGANIZATION

Priority	Ministry Goal/Action	Date	Amount	Amt. Youth Will Pay

44

Personal Project Planning

My worst fears were realized as I turned the calendar page to the next month. A major project was scheduled for the first weekend, and I had not prepared for it ahead of time! After barely surviving the ordeal of making last-minute arrangements, I began working on a process of personal planning to avoid this situation in the future.

This process of project planning is built around two planning forms. You will need several copies of form 1 (at least one for each event to be planned). You will need about fifty-two copies of form 2 (one per week for a year).

Prepare the Forms

You need a desk calendar for planning. Number all the Mondays in the year beginning with the first Monday in January and continuing through the last Monday in December. Fill in the dates and week numbers on the fifty-two copies of form 2.

Look through your youth ministry calendar and identify every major event that needs to be included in your personal planning. Fill in the top part of form 1 for every major event. Put the target date and the week number of each event on a form.

Begin the Planning

Select one of the major projects and begin brainstorming *every action* that needs to be done to complete the project. List these under the column "Planning-Preparation Strategies" on the copy of form 1 for that project. Do not miss any detail in the steps that need to be done.

Project Due Dates

Look over the list of steps and estimate the number of weeks ahead of time each step should be completed. Write this in the first column to the right of the step. For example, when planning a youth retreat, the location for the retreat should be secured six months (twenty-six

BACK TO SCHOOL RETREAT
Project

SEPTEMBER 3, 19XX	**#36**
(target date)	(Week of Activity #1)

PLANNING-PREPARATION STRATEGIES:	Due Date in Weeks Prior to Target Date	Calendar Week No. When Strategy To Be Performed
☐ RESERVE LOCATION	26	10
☐ ENLIST COUNSELORS	13	213
☐ CHOOSE THEME	8	28
☐ _____		
☐ _____		
☐ (ETC.)		
☐		
☐		
☐		
☐		
☐		
☐		
☐		
☐		
☐		
☐		
☐		
☐		
☐		

CALENDAR WEEK # _____

_____

(dates)

THINGS TO BE DONE THIS WEEK:

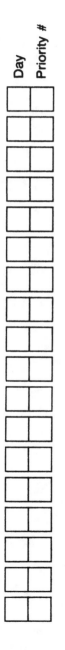

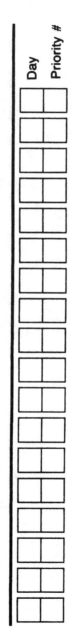

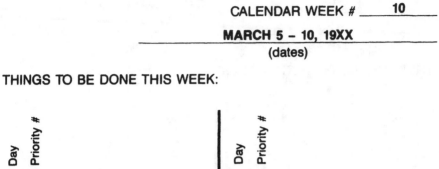

CALENDAR WEEK # _____10_____

MARCH 5 – 10, 19XX
(dates)

THINGS TO BE DONE THIS WEEK:

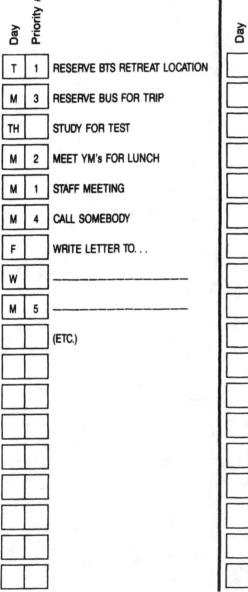

Day	Priority #	
T	1	RESERVE BTS RETREAT LOCATION
M	3	RESERVE BUS FOR TRIP
TH		STUDY FOR TEST
M	2	MEET YM's FOR LUNCH
M	1	STAFF MEETING
M	4	CALL SOMEBODY
F		WRITE LETTER TO. . .
W		————————
M	5	————————
		(ETC.)

Project

_____

(target date)

(Week of Activity #1)

PLANNING-PREPARATION STRATEGIES:

	Due Date in Weeks Prior to Target Date	Calendar Week No. When Strategy To Be Performed
☐		
☐		
☐		
☐		
☐		
☐		
☐		
☐		
☐		
☐		
☐		
☐		
☐		
☐		
☐		
☐		
☐		
☐		
☐		

weeks) ahead of time. Write the number *26* in the column beside "secure retreat location."

The next step involves a little math, but it helps to firm up the due dates for each planning step. For each step you listed on form 1, subtract the number in the first column from the week number of the event (written at the top of the form). Write this number in the second column on the right side of the form. This number represents the week number on your desk calendar when the action must be done. This is also the number that will be used on form 2 for your weekly planning lists.

Prepare Weekly Lists

Using all the copies of form 2 (weekly lists) transfer the steps in the planning for each major project (on form 1) to their appropriate week (on form 2). For example, the week number listed in the far right column in our example is 10. The planning step is "secure retreat location." On form 2 for week number 10, write "secure retreat location" on the list of things to do that week. Work through all the steps, listing every action to be done on the appropriate week listed on form 1.

Prioritize Weekly Lists

On Monday morning, turn to the copy of form 2 for that week and look over the list of things to do. It might contain planning steps for several major projects along with other things to be done. List additional tasks that you need to do during the week.

Then decide which day to complete the tasks. Assign priority numbers to tasks when there is more than one per day. The result is a list of tasks to be completed that week. If these are completed on time, the planning for all major events will progress on time, and many problems will be avoided.

Watch out for holidays, vacation times, other major assignments, and times when you will be out of the office for extended times. If you are at summer youth camp, it will be difficult to work on planning tasks for an event in the fall. Write down the dates you will be gone and adjust your planning accordingly.

Quarterly Planning

One additional form has been helpful in visualizing the entire youth ministry for an extended period of time. The Quarterly Planning Form gives a summary of the youth education, socials, recreation, and ministry.

The column along the left side of this form represents the weeks of the quarter. Each column represents a major program or planning area of youth ministry.

First, use the printed curriculum materials to fill in the units of study for Bible study, discipleship training, and missions education. Use the weeks along the left to indicate the beginning date for each study.

Then fill in music the youth choir will be performing. Also, list major social events (banquet, party, hayride, or so forth) under the Fellowship column. Under Recreation list all outdoor sports and activities (basketball games, sports leagues, campouts, and so forth).

Then fill in the remainder of the plan sheet. Keeping in mind the ongoing program organizations, list studies or emphases for a Wednesday night or weekday Bible study with youth to enhance the ongoing studies. For example, if youth are studying Old Testament passages on Sunday morning, use material from the New Testament or a character or topical study for weekday studies. The blank column on the right side can be used to list churchwide events that will impact the youth ministry planning.

This Quarterly Planning Sheet provides a quick, concise picture of the total scope of youth ministry programming on one sheet. Place this sheet in the front of your calendar or plan book for quick easy reference.

Quarterly Planning Form

WK.	Bible Study	Discipleship Training	Week-Night Activities	Music	Missions Education	Recreation	Fellowship	
1								
2								
3								
4								
5								
6								
7								
8								
9								
10								
11								
12								
13								

Appendix 1. Job Description for Minister of Youth

The following is a sample job description suitable for a full-time youth minister. Some adaptations be needed because of different staff arrangements or different church situations.

Principal Function

The minister of youth is responsible to the pastor (or minister of education) for leading the church to develop a comprehensive youth ministry. This will be done in consultation with other staff members and church program organizations concerning activities, policies, and procedures that relate to their areas of responsibility.

Responsibilities

1. Work in cooperation with organizational leaders to plan, implement, and evaluate a comprehensive youth ministry.
2. Conduct meetings with youth when needed or when appropriate to enhance the work of the church program organizations.
3. Work in cooperation with appropriate persons, including the nominating committee in selecting, enlisting, training, supervising, and counseling with youth leaders in the church program organizations.
4. Provide special training opportunities for youth leaders in cooperation with the church's overall training effort.
5. Advise the use of program materials, curriculum resources, equipment, supplies, and space by youth groups in all church program organizations.
6. Assist youth leaders in locating and using media and recreation equipment and supplies.
7. Coordinate the planning of special projects and activities (such as youth camps, retreats, mission trips, and fellowships) with church program organizations.
8. Work with youth leaders to coordinate visitation for the youth division and lead youth leaders to visit prospects and absentees.
9. Plan and conduct meetings when needed or when appropriate for parents of youth.

10. Assist the pastor in pastoral counseling, advice, and appropriate referrals in relation to problems encountered by youth and their families.
11. Prepare and administer the youth ministry budget.
12. Stay informed about denominational goals, emphases, publications, materials, and plans as they relate to the local church and its programs.
13. Stay informed about current youth education methods, materials, promotional ideas, youth trends, and administration techniques, utilizing them where appropriate.
14. Perform other ministerial duties as assigned to support the total work of the church.

Appendix 2. Job Description for Youth Ministry Coordinator

The following is a sample job description suitable for a part-time or volunteer youth minister. Some adaptations may be needed because of different staff arrangements or different church situations.

Principal Function

The youth ministry coordinator is responsible to the pastor for planning, coordinating, promoting, and evaluating the church's youth ministry.

Responsibilities

1. Coordinate the total youth education effort within the following areas: Sunday School, discipleship programs, missions education groups, weekday programs, and Wednesday night prayer/ Bible study.
2. Enlist youth leaders in cooperation with the church nominating committee. Promote and develop youth leadership training.
3. Give guidance and counsel through organizational channels to volunteer leaders with youth.
4. Lead youth leaders in a systematic plan of evangelism and outreach.
5. Cooperate with the music director in correlating a program of music activities related to youth.
6. Cooperate with church program organization leaders in planning and conducting recreational activities with youth.
7. Serve as a member of the church council. Work with the youth ministry council.
8. Meet with parents of youth when needed or appropriate for the purpose of information and input related to youth ministry.
9. Assist in preparing budget requests for the youth ministry.
10. Stay informed of the latest youth work materials and methods.
11. Buy and maintain youth supplies within budget allocations.

Appendix 3. Job Description for Minister of Music and Youth

The following is a sample job description for a person serving as a combination minister of music and youth. Some adaptations may be needed because of different staff arrangements or different church situations.

Principal Function

The minister of music and youth is responsible to the pastor for (1) developing and promoting the total music program of the church, and (2) coordinating the work of the youth program organizations in developing a comprehensive youth ministry. This will be done in cooperation with other staff members and appropriate leaders concerning activities, policies, and procedures that relate to their areas of responsibility.

Responsibilities

1. Direct the planning, coordinating, conducting, and evaluating of comprehensive music and youth ministry programs based on program tasks.
2. Work in cooperation with appropriate persons, including the nominating committee in selecting, enlisting, training, supervising, and counseling with youth leaders in the church program organizations and music leaders in the total music program.
3. Supervise the work of assigned paid staff workers.
4. Serve as a member of the church council. Coordinate the music and youth ministries with the organizational calendar and emphases of the church.
5. Assist the pastor in planning all services of worship.
6. Lead in planning and promoting the choir program; direct and coordinate the work of volunteer choir leaders; direct or coordinate the work of adult, youth, and children's, and other music groups as needed.
7. Give direction to a music ministry plan of visitation. Work with organizational leaders to coordinate visitation for the youth division and lead workers to visit prospects and absentees.

8. Arrange and provide music for weddings, funerals, special projects, and other church-related activities upon request.
9. Maintain music library, materials, supplies, musical instruments, and other music equipment.
10. Stay informed about current music methods, materials, promotion, and administration. Stay informed about current youth educational methods, materials, promotional ideas, and administrative techniques, utilizing them where appropriate.
11. Conduct special training projects for youth leaders in proper relationship to the church's training effort.
12. Plan and conduct meetings when needed or appropriate for parents of youth.
13. Advise in the use of program materials, equipment, supplies, and space by youth groups in all church program organizations.
14. Conduct meetings with youth when needed or appropriate to enhance the work of the church program organizations.
15. Coordinate the planning of special projects and activities (such as youth camps, mission trips, youth choir tours, retreats, and fellowships) with youth program organizations.
16. Prepare and administer the budgets for the music and youth ministries.
17. Be informed about denominational goals, emphases, publications, materials, and plans for employing them as they relate to the local church and its programs.
18. Perform other ministerial duties as assigned to support the total work of the church.

Notes

Part 1

1. *Interpreter's Dictionary of the Bible*, vol. 3 K-Q, "Christian Ministry" (Nashville: Abingdon Press, 1962), 386.

2. Art Criscoe, *Youth Becoming Leaders* (Nashville: Convention Press, 1984), 19.

3. Bob Taylor, *The Youth Ministry Planbook* (Nashville: Convention Press, 1977), 2.

4. Adapted from Wesley Black, "Shared Planning," in *Youth Ministry Planbook 4*, comp. by Richard Ross (Nashville: Convention Press, 1989), 10-13.

5. Peter Benson, Dorothy Williams, and Arthur Johnson, *The Quicksilver Years* (San Francisco: Harper and Row, 1987), 27.

Part 2

1. Adapted from *Youth Leadership Training Pak Guidebook* (Nashville: Convention Press, 1982), 12-13.

2. Ibid., 6.

3. Reginald M. McDonough, *Keys to Effective Motivation* (Nashville: Broadman Press, 1979), 71-78.

4. Reginald M. McDonough, *Working with Volunteer Leaders in the Church*, (Nashville: Broadman Press, 1979), 132.

5. Ibid., 135-41.

Part 3

1. "Youth Population and Sunday School Enrollment Trends," handout from Sunday School Division, BSSB, based on U. S. Department of Commerce Bureau of Census Information, U. S. Population Trends 1983-2080.

2. Peter Benson, Dorothy Williams, and Arthur Johnson, *The Quicksilver Years* (San Francisco: Harper and Row, 1987), 111.

3. Robert J. Havighurst, *Developmental Tasks and Education* (New York: Longman, Green, 1951).

4. Erik Erikson, *Childhood and Society* (New York: W. W. Norton, 1950).

5. Erik Erikson, *Identity: Youth and Crisis* (New York: W. W. Norton, 1968), 22.

6. Merton P. Strommen and A. Irene Strommen, *Five Cries of Parents* (San Francisco: Harper and Row, 1985), 33-34. Adapted from John Hill, *Understanding Early Adolescence* (Carboro: Center for Early Adolescence, University of North Carolina, 1980).

7. Barbara Forisha-Kovach, *The Experience of Adolescence* (Glenview, Ill.: Scott, Foresman and Company, 1983), 100.

8. Roberta G. Simmons and Dale A. Blyth, *Moving Into Adolescence* (New York: Aldine D. Gruyter, 1987), 162.

9. Ibid., 195.

10. Benson, Williams, and Johnson, 63.

11. Ibid., 64.

12. Ibid., 67.

13. Ibid., 68.

240

14. Ibid., 27-30.

15. "World Youth Survey Results," *TeenAge Magazine*, April/May, 1986, 52-53, cited in Eugene C. Roehlkepartain, ed., *The Youth Ministry Resource Book* (Loveland, Colo.: Group Books, 1988), 32.

16. Karen S. Peterson, "Whom Do You Turn To?" *USA Today*, May 26, 1987, 6D, cited in Roehlkepartain, 32.

17. John J. Conger and Anne C. Petersen, *Adolescence and Youth*, 3d ed. (New York: Harper and Row, 1984), 330.

18. Adapted from David Elkind, *All Grown Up and No Place to Go* (Reading, Mass.: Addison-Wesley, 1984), 200-06.

19. Ibid., 205.

20. Benson, Williams, and Johnson, 25.

21. Ibid., 55-56.

22. Ibid., 58.

23. L. J. Stone and J. Church, *Childhood and Adolescence: A Psychology of the Growing Person*, 3d ed. (New York: Random House, 1973), 442, quoted in Conger and Petersen, 333.

24. Elkind, 69-70.

25. Ibid., 23.

26. B. Inhelder and J. Piaget, *The Growth of Logical Thinking from Childhood to Adolescence* (New York: Basic Books, 1958), summarized in Conger and Petersen, 158-64.

27. David Elkind, "Understanding the Younger Adolescent," *Adolescence* 13 (Spring 1978): 128.

28. Ibid., 129-30.

29. James W. Fowler, *Stages of Faith* (San Francisco: Harper and Row, 1981).

30. Daniel O. Aleshire, *Understanding Today's Youth* (Nashville: Convention Press, 1982), 113.

31. Ibid., 113-15.

32. Ibid., 113.

33. Strommen and Strommen, 72-73.

34. Benson, Williams, and Johnson, 220.

35. Roland D. Martinson, *Effective Youth Ministry* (Minneapolis: Augsburg, 1988), 39.

36. Strommen and Strommen, 147.

37. Ibid., 86.

38. Benson, Williams, and Johnson, 163.

39. Mark H. Senter II, "Axioms of Youth Ministry," in Warren S. Benson and Mark H. Senter III, *The Complete Book of Youth Ministry* (Chicago: Moody Press, 1987), 216.

40. Benson, Williams, and Johnson, 201.

41. Aleshire, 104.

42. Barbara B. Varenhorst and Lee Sparks, *Training Teenagers for Peer Ministry* (Loveland, Colo.: Group Books, 1988), 14.

43. Ibid., 10.

44. Merton P. Strommen, "Future Trends Affecting Youth Ministry," *Search* 17 (Summer 1987): 38.

45. Varenhorst, 9.

46. Susan Chase, "My Generation," *Seventeen*, October 1989, 106.

47. Roehlkepartain, 19.

48. Ibid., 23.

49. Ibid., 21-23.

Part 4

1. Peter Benson, Dorothy Williams, and Arthur Johnson, *The Quicksilver Years* (San Francisco: Harper and Row, 1987), 214.

2. Laurence Steinberg, *Adolescence* (New York: Alfred A. Knopf, 1985), 129-30.

3. Merton P. Strommen and A. Irene Strommen, *Five Cries of Parents* (San Francisco: Harper and Row, 1985), 16.

4. Tony Campolo, "The Death of Traditional Parenthood," *Youthworker,* Spring 1985, 42.

5. Robert J. Havighurst, *Developmental Tasks and Education,* 3d ed. (New York: David McKay Co., 1972), 95-106.

6. Barbara Smith, "Adolescent and Parent: Interaction Between Developmental Stages," *Center Quarterly Focus,* (Minneapolis: Center for Youth Development and Research, 1976), 2-9.

7. Benson, Williams, and Johnson, 212.

8. Strommen and Strommen, 88-89.

9. Ibid., 90

10. Richard Ross and G. Wade Rowatt, Jr., *Ministry with Youth and Their Parents* (Nashville: Convention Press, 1986), 43-52.

11. Strommen and Strommen, 147.

12. H. L. Hodgkinson, "The Patterns of Our Social Fabric are Changing," *Education Week,* May 14, 1986, cited in Merton P. Strommen, *Five Cries of Youth, Revised* (San Francisco: Harper and Row, 1988), 64.

13. Eugene Roehlkepartain, ed., *The Youth Ministry Resource Book* (Loveland, Colo.: Group Books, 1988), 30.

14. Benson, Williams, and Johnson, 197.

15. Richard Ross, *Youth Ministry Planbook 3* (Nashville: Convention Press, 1985), 22.

Part 5

1. Frances Anderson, "The Pastor: Key to Effective Youth Ministry," *Affirmation* 2: (Spring 1989): 85.

2. Wesley Black, "A Comparison of Responses to Learning Objectives for Youth Discipleship Training from Ministers of Youth in Southern Baptist Churches and Students Enrolled in Youth Education Courses at Southwestern Baptist Theological Seminary" (Ed.D. diss., Southwestern Baptist Theological Seminary, 1985), 59.

3. Ibid., 60

4. *The Youth Ministry ResourceBook* (Loveland, Colo.: Thom Schultz Publications, 1988), 184.

Part 6

1. Richard Ross, "The Effect of Teaching Methodology as Presented in the Southern Baptist Curriculum Base Design on Selected Attitudes Related to Mate Selection Among High School Students" (Ed.D. diss., Southwestern Baptist Theological Seminary, 1981), 87.

2. *Church Base Design 1986 Update,* (Nashville: The Sunday School Board of the Southern Baptist Convention, 1986), 2, 51.

3. Adapted from Richard Ross, comp., *Youth Ministry Planbook 4,* (Nashville: Convention Press, 1989), 16-17.